CROCK·POT

Family Favorite
Recipes

pil

Publications International, Ltd.

Contents

Slow Cooking 101

Slow Cooker Sizes

Smaller **CROCK-POT®** slow cookers—such as 1- to 3½-quart models—are the perfect size for cooking for singles, a couple or empty-nesters (and also for serving dips).

While medium-size **CROCK-POT®** slow cookers (those holding somewhere between 3 quarts and 5 quarts) will easily cook enough food at a time to feed a small family, they're also convenient for holiday side dishes or appetizers.

Large **CROCK-POT®** slow cookers are great for large family dinners, holiday entertaining and potluck suppers. A 6- to 7-quart model is ideal if you like to make meals in advance, or have dinner tonight and store leftovers for another day.

Types of Slow Cookers

Current **CROCK-POT®** slow cookers come equipped with many different features and benefits, from auto cook programs to stovetop-safe stoneware to timed programming. Visit **WWW.CROCK-POT.COM** to find the **CROCK-POT®** slow cooker that best suits your needs.

How you plan to use a **CROCK-POT®** slow cooker may affect the model you choose to purchase. For everyday cooking, choose a size large enough to serve your family. If you plan to use the **CROCK-POT®** slow cooker primarily for entertaining, choose one of the larger sizes. Basic **CROCK-POT®** slow cookers can hold as little as 16 ounces or as much as 7 quarts. The smallest sizes are great for keeping dips warm on a buffet, while the larger sizes can more readily fit large quantities of food and larger roasts.

Cooking, Stirring and Food Safety

CROCK-POT® slow cookers are safe to leave unattended. The outer heating base may get hot as it cooks, but it should not pose a fire hazard. The heating element in the heating base functions at a low wattage and is safe for your countertops.

Your **CROCK-POT®** slow cooker should be filled about one-half to three-fourths full for most recipes unless otherwise instructed. Lean meats such as chicken or pork tenderloin will cook faster than meats with more connective tissue and fat such as beef chuck or pork shoulder. Bone-in meats will take longer than boneless cuts. Typical **CROCK-POT®** slow cooker dishes take approximately 7 to 8 hours to reach the simmer point on LOW and about 3 to 4 hours on HIGH. Once the vegetables and meat start to simmer and braise, their flavors will fully blend and meat will become fall-off-the-bone tender.

According to the USDA, all bacteria are killed at a temperature of 165°F. It's important to follow the recommended cooking times and not to open the lid often, especially early in the cooking process when heat is building up inside the unit. If you need to open the lid to check on your food or are adding additional ingredients, remember to allow additional cooking time if necessary to ensure food is cooked through and tender.

Large **CROCK-POT®** slow cookers, the 6- to 7-quart sizes, may benefit with a quick stir halfway through cook time to help distribute heat and promote even cooking. It's usually unnecessary to stir at all, as even ½ cup liquid will help to distribute heat, and the stoneware is the perfect medium for holding food at an even temperature throughout the cooking process.

Oven-Safe

All **CROCK-POT®** slow cooker removable stoneware inserts may (without their lids) be used safely in ovens at up to 400°F. Also, all **CROCK-POT®** slow cookers are microwavable without their lids. If you own another brand of slow cooker, please refer to your owner's manual for specific stoneware cooking medium tolerances.

Frozen Food

Frozen food or partially frozen food can be successfully cooked in a **CROCK-POT®** slow cooker; however, it will require longer cooking time than the same recipe made with fresh food. It's almost always preferable to thaw frozen food prior to placing it in the **CROCK-POT®** slow cooker. Using an instant-read thermometer is recommended to ensure meat is fully cooked through.

Pasta and Rice

If you're converting a recipe that calls for uncooked pasta, cook the pasta on the stovetop just until slightly tender before adding to the **CROCK-POT®** slow cooker. If you are converting a recipe that calls for cooked rice, stir in raw rice with other ingredients; add ¼ cup extra liquid per ¼ cup of raw rice.

Beans

Beans must be softened completely before combining with sugar and/or acidic foods. Sugar and acid have a hardening effect on beans and will prevent softening. Fully cooked canned beans may be used as a substitute for dried beans.

Vegetables

Root vegetables often cook more slowly than meat. Cut vegetables accordingly to cook at the same rate as meat—large versus small, or lean versus marbled—and place near the sides or bottom of the stoneware to facilitate cooking.

Herbs

Fresh herbs add flavor and color when added at the end of the cooking cycle; if added at the beginning, many fresh herbs' flavor will dissipate over long cook times. Ground and/or dried herbs and spices work well in slow cooking and may be added at the beginning, and for dishes with shorter cook times, hearty fresh herbs such as rosemary and thyme hold up well. The flavor power of all herbs and spices can vary greatly depending on their particular strength and shelf life. Use chili powders and garlic powder sparingly, as these can sometimes intensify over the long cook times. Always taste the finished dish and correct seasonings including salt and pepper.

Liquids

It is not necessary to use more than ½ to 1 cup liquid in most instances since juices in meats and vegetables are retained more in slow cooking than in conventional cooking. Excess liquid can be cooked down and concentrated after slow cooking on the stovetop or by removing meat and vegetables from the stoneware, stirring in one of the following thickeners, and setting the slow cooker to HIGH. Cook on HIGH for approximately 15 minutes or until juices are thickened.

FLOUR: All-purpose flour is often used to thicken soups or stews. Stir cold water into the flour in a small bowl until smooth. With the **CROCK-POT**® slow cooker on HIGH, whisk the flour mixture into the liquid in the **CROCK-POT**® slow cooker. Cover; cook on HIGH 15 minutes or until the mixture is thickened.

CORNSTARCH: Cornstarch gives sauces a clear, shiny appearance; it's used most often for sweet dessert sauces and stir-fry sauces. Stir cold water into the cornstarch in a small bowl until the cornstarch dissolves.

Quickly stir this mixture into the liquid in the **CROCK-POT**® slow cooker; the sauce will thicken as soon as the liquid boils. Cornstarch breaks down with too much heat, so never add it at the beginning of the slow cooking process, and turn off the heat as soon as the sauce thickens.

ARROWROOT: Arrowroot (or arrowroot flour) comes from the root of a tropical plant that is dried and ground to a powder; it produces a thick, clear sauce. Those who are allergic to wheat often use it in place of flour. Place arrowroot in a small bowl or cup and stir in cold water until the mixture is smooth. Quickly stir this mixture into the liquid in the **CROCK-POT**® slow cooker. Arrowroot thickens below the boiling point, so it even works well in a **CROCK-POT**® slow cooker on LOW. Too much stirring can break down an arrowroot mixture.

TAPIOCA: Tapioca is a starchy substance extracted from the root of the cassava plant. Its greatest advantage is that it withstands long cooking, making it an ideal choice for slow cooking. Add it at the beginning of cooking and you'll get a clear, thickened sauce in the finished dish. Dishes using tapioca as a thickener are best cooked on the LOW setting; tapioca may become stringy when boiled for a long time.

Milk

Milk, cream and sour cream break down during extended cooking. When possible, add them during the last 15 to 30 minutes of cooking, until just heated through. Condensed soups may be substituted for milk and can cook for extended times.

Fish

Fish is delicate and should be stirred in gently during the last 15 to 30 minutes of cooking time. Cover and cook just until cooked through and serve immediately.

Baked Goods

If you wish to prepare bread, cakes or pudding cakes in a **CROCK-POT**® slow cooker, you may want to purchase a covered, vented metal cake pan accessory for your **CROCK-POT**® slow cooker. You can also use any straight-sided soufflé dish or deep cake pan that will fit into the stoneware of your unit. Baked goods can be prepared directly in the stoneware; however, they can be a little difficult to remove from the insert, so follow the recipe directions carefully.

Rise and Shine

Roasted Pepper and Sourdough Egg Dish

Makes 6 servings

- **3** cups sourdough bread cubes
- **1** jar (12 ounces) roasted red pepper strips, drained
- **1** cup (4 ounces) shredded Monterey Jack cheese
- **1** cup (4 ounces) shredded sharp Cheddar cheese
- **1** cup cottage cheese
- **6** eggs
- **1** cup milk
- **¼** cup chopped fresh cilantro
- **¼** teaspoon black pepper

1 Coat inside of **CROCK-POT**® slow cooker with nonstick cooking spray. Add bread. Arrange roasted peppers evenly over bread cubes; sprinkle with Monterey Jack and Cheddar cheeses.

2 Place cottage cheese in food processor or blender; process until smooth. Add eggs and milk; process just until blended. Stir in cilantro and black pepper.

3 Pour egg mixture into **CROCK-POT**® slow cooker. Cover; cook on LOW 3 to 3½ hours or on HIGH 2 to 2½ hours or until eggs are firm but still moist.

Overnight Breakfast Porridge

Makes 4 servings

- ¾ cup steel-cut oats
- ¼ cup uncooked quinoa, rinsed and drained
- ¼ cup dried cranberries, plus additional for serving
- ¼ cup raisins
- 3 tablespoons ground flax seeds
- 2 tablespoons chia seeds
- ¼ teaspoon ground cinnamon
- 2½ cups almond milk, plus additional for serving
- Maple syrup (optional)
- ¼ cup sliced almonds, toasted*

*To toast almonds, spread in single layer in heavy skillet. Cook and stir over medium heat 1 to 2 minutes or until nuts are lightly browned.

1 Combine oats, quinoa, ¼ cup cranberries, raisins, flax seeds, chia seeds and cinnamon in heat-safe bowl that fits inside of 5- or 6-quart **CROCK-POT®** slow cooker. Stir in 2½ cups almond milk.

2 Place bowl in **CROCK-POT®** slow cooker; pour enough water to come halfway up side of bowl.

3 Cover; cook on LOW 8 hours. Carefully remove bowl from **CROCK-POT®** slow cooker. Stir in additional almond milk, if desired. Top each serving with maple syrup, almonds and additional cranberries, if desired.

Hawaiian Bread French Toast

Makes 8 to 10 servings

6 **eggs**

1 **cup milk**

1 **cup whipping cream**

¼ **cup sugar**

2 **teaspoons coconut extract**

2 **teaspoons vanilla**

1 **teaspoon ground cinnamon**

1 **pound sweet Hawaiian rolls or bread, sliced lengthwise and cut to fit CROCK-POT® slow cooker**

2 **tablespoons unsalted butter, cut into ¼-inch pieces**

½ **cup flaked coconut, toasted***

*To toast coconut, spread in single layer in heavy-bottomed skillet. Cook and stir over medium heat 1 to 2 minutes or until lightly browned. Remove from skillet immediately. Cool before using.

1 Coat inside of **CROCK-POT®** slow cooker with nonstick cooking spray. Whisk eggs, milk, cream, sugar, coconut extract, vanilla and cinnamon in large bowl.

2 Place bread in **CROCK-POT®** slow cooker; sprinkle butter over top. Pour egg mixture on top; press bread down to absorb egg mixture. Cover; cook on HIGH 2 hours. Sprinkle with toasted coconut.

Denver Egg Bowls

Makes 4 servings

4 bell peppers, any color

10 eggs

¼ cup diced ham, plus additional for topping

3 green onions, chopped

1 cup (4 ounces) shredded Cheddar cheese

1 Cut thin slice off top of each bell pepper; reserve tops. Carefully remove and discard seeds and membranes, leaving peppers whole. Dice bell pepper tops; measure ¼ cup. Discard remaining diced bell pepper or reserve for another use.

2 Whisk eggs, ¼ cup diced bell peppers, ¼ cup ham and green onions in large measuring cup until well blended. Pour egg mixture evenly into each bell pepper; place in **CROCK-POT**® slow cooker. Fill **CROCK-POT**® slow cooker with water about three fourths up bell peppers.

3 Cover; cook on HIGH 3½ hours. Sprinkle with cheese and additional ham, if desired.

Breakfast Nests

Makes 4 servings

1 package (12 ounces) frozen butternut squash spirals, thawed

1 teaspoon vegetable oil

¼ teaspoon salt, plus additional for serving

¼ teaspoon ground nutmeg

¼ teaspoon black pepper, plus additional for serving

4 eggs

1 Line four 6- to 8-ounce ramekins with square of parchment paper; spray parchment with nonstick cooking spray.

2 Combine butternut squash spirals, oil, ¼ teaspoon salt, nutmeg and ¼ teaspoon pepper in medium bowl; toss to coat. Arrange butternut squash spirals evenly in nests in prepared ramekins. Crack one egg over squash in each ramekin. Fill **CROCK-POT®** slow cooker with ¼-inch water; add ramekins.

3 Cover; cook on HIGH 2 hours or until whites are set and yolks are desired doneness. Remove nests from ramekins using parchment to plates, if desired. Season with additional salt and pepper.

Maple Pumpkin Butter

Makes 4 cups

2 cans (about 15 ounces *each*) pumpkin purée

¾ cup packed dark brown sugar

¼ cup maple syrup

1 teaspoon ground cinnamon

½ teaspoon ground ginger

¼ teaspoon ground cloves

¼ teaspoon ground allspice

¼ teaspoon ground nutmeg

⅛ teaspoon salt

1 tablespoon lemon juice

1 Combine pumpkin purée, brown sugar, maple syrup, cinnamon, ginger, cloves, allspice, nutmeg and salt in **CROCK-POT®** slow cooker; stir to blend. Cover; cook on LOW 7 hours or on HIGH 3½ hours, stirring every 2 to 3 hours.

2 Stir in lemon juice. Divide among storage containers; cool completely. Cover; refrigerate up to 3 weeks.

Cranberry Orange Scones

Makes 6 servings

¼ cup (½ stick) cold butter

1 cup plus 2 tablespoons self-rising flour, divided

¾ cup buttermilk

2 teaspoons granulated sugar

¼ cup dried cranberries

1½ teaspoons orange peel, divided

½ teaspoon ground cinnamon

¼ cup powdered sugar

1½ teaspoons orange juice

⅛ teaspoon salt

1 Cut one 16-inch piece of parchment paper; fold in half crosswise. Fit parchment paper into bottom and partly up sides of 1½-quart **CROCK-POT**® slow cooker. Coat parchment paper with nonstick cooking spray.

2 Grate cold butter into medium bowl. Add 1 cup flour, buttermilk and granulated sugar; stir until dry ingredients are just moistened. *Do not overmix.* Combine cranberries, 1 teaspoon orange peel and cinnamon in small bowl; toss to coat. Fold cranberry mixture into dough.

3 Sprinkle work surface with remaining 2 tablespoons flour. Place dough onto work surface; knead briefly until dough forms a ball. Press into 6-inch disc; score into six wedges. Place disc into **CROCK-POT**® slow cooker on top of parchment paper.

4 Lay a clean kitchen towel across top of **CROCK-POT**® slow cooker; cover with lid. Cover; cook on HIGH 1½ hours. Remove scones with parchment paper to wire rack. Combine powdered sugar, orange juice, remaining ½ teaspoon orange peel and salt in small bowl; whisk until blended. Drizzle over scones; serve warm or at room temperature.

Overnight Bacon, Sourdough, Egg and Cheese Casserole

Makes 6 servings

1 loaf (about 12 ounces) sourdough bread, cut into ¾-inch cubes

8 slices thick-cut bacon, chopped

1 large onion, chopped

1 medium red bell pepper, chopped

1 medium green bell pepper, chopped

2 teaspoons dried oregano

¼ cup sun-dried tomatoes packed in oil, drained and chopped

1½ cups (6 ounces) shredded sharp Cheddar cheese, divided

10 eggs

1 cup milk

1 teaspoon salt

¾ teaspoon black pepper

1 Coat inside of **CROCK-POT**® slow cooker with nonstick cooking spray. Add bread. Heat large skillet over medium heat. Add bacon; cook 7 to 9 minutes or until crisp. Remove bacon to paper towel-lined plate using slotted spoon. Pour off all but 1 tablespoon of drippings from skillet. Heat same skillet over medium heat. Add onion, bell peppers and oregano; cook 5 to 7 minutes or until onion is softened, stirring occasionally. Stir in sun-dried tomatoes; cook 1 minute. Pour over bread in **CROCK-POT**® slow cooker. Stir in bacon and 1 cup cheese.

2 Beat eggs, milk, salt and black pepper in large bowl; pour over bread mixture in **CROCK-POT**® slow cooker. Press down on bread to allow bread mixture to absorb egg mixture. Sprinkle remaining ½ cup cheese over top. Cover; cook on LOW 6 to 8 hours or on HIGH 3½ to 4 hours. Cut into squares to serve.

Hawaiian Fruit Compote

Makes 6 to 8 servings

3 cups coarsely chopped fresh pineapple

3 grapefruits, peeled and sectioned

1 can (21 ounces) cherry pie filling

2 cups chopped fresh peaches

2 to 3 limes, peeled and sectioned

1 mango, peeled and chopped

2 bananas, sliced

1 tablespoon lemon juice

Prepared waffles (optional)

Slivered almonds

Fresh mint sprigs (optional)

Combine pineapple, grapefruits, pie filling, peaches, limes, mango, bananas and lemon juice in **CROCK-POT®** slow cooker; toss to blend. Cover; cook on LOW 4 to 5 hours or on HIGH 2 to 3 hours. Top waffles with compote, if desired. Sprinkle with almonds. Garnish with mint.

SERVING SUGGESTIONS: Try warm, fruity compote in place of maple syrup on your favorite morning foods. This sauce is also delicious served over baked ham.

Blueberry-Banana Pancakes

Makes 8 servings

2 cups all-purpose flour

⅓ cup sugar

1 tablespoon baking powder

½ teaspoon baking soda

½ teaspoon salt

½ teaspoon ground cinnamon

1¾ cups milk

2 eggs, lightly beaten

¼ cup (½ stick) unsalted butter, melted

1 teaspoon vanilla

1 cup fresh blueberries

2 small bananas, sliced

Maple syrup (optional)

1 Coat inside of **CROCK-POT**® slow cooker with nonstick cooking spray. Combine flour, sugar, baking powder, baking soda, salt and cinnamon in large bowl; stir to blend. Combine milk, eggs, butter and vanilla in medium bowl; whisk to blend. Pour milk mixture into flour mixture; stir until dry ingredients are moistened. Gently fold in blueberries until mixed. Pour batter into **CROCK-POT**® slow cooker.

2 Cover; cook on HIGH 2 hours or until puffed and toothpick inserted into center comes out clean. Cut evenly into eight wedges; top with sliced bananas and maple syrup, if desired.

Bran Muffin Bread

Makes 1 loaf

¼ cup (½ stick) unsalted butter, melted, plus additional for mold and foil

2 cups whole wheat flour, plus additional for mold*

2 cups all-bran cereal

2 teaspoons baking powder

1 teaspoon baking soda

¼ teaspoon ground cinnamon

½ teaspoon salt

1 egg

1½ cups buttermilk

¼ cup molasses

1 cup chopped walnuts

½ cup raisins

Honey (optional)

*For proper texture of the finished bread, spoon flour into measuring cup and level off. Do not dip into bag, pack down flour or tap on counter to level when measuring.

1 Butter and flour 8-cup mold that fits inside of 6-quart **CROCK-POT®** slow cooker. Combine cereal, 2 cups flour, baking powder, baking soda, cinnamon and salt in large bowl.

2 Beat egg in medium bowl. Whisk in buttermilk, molasses and ¼ cup melted butter. Stir into flour mixture just until combined. Stir in walnuts and raisins. Spoon batter into prepared mold. Cover with buttered foil, butter side down.

3 Place rack in **CROCK-POT®** slow cooker. Pour 1 inch hot water into **CROCK-POT®** slow cooker (water should not come to top of rack). Place mold on rack. Cover; cook on LOW 3½ to 4 hours or until bread starts to pull away from side of mold and toothpick inserted into center comes out clean.

4 Remove mold from **CROCK-POT®** slow cooker. Let stand 10 minutes. Remove foil and run rubber spatula around outer edge, lifting bottom slightly to loosen. Invert bread onto wire rack. Serve warm with honey, if desired.

 Tip Cooking times are guidelines. **CROCK-POT®** slow cookers, just like ovens, cook differently depending on the recipe size and the individual **CROCK-POT®** slow cooker. Always check for doneness before serving.

Bacon and Cheese Brunch Potatoes

Makes 6 servings

3 medium russet potatoes (about 2 pounds), cut into 1-inch cubes

1 cup chopped onion

½ teaspoon seasoned salt

4 slices bacon, crisp-cooked and crumbled

1 cup (4 ounces) shredded sharp Cheddar cheese

1 tablespoon water

1 Coat inside of **CROCK-POT®** slow cooker with nonstick cooking spray. Place half of potatoes in **CROCK-POT®** slow cooker. Sprinkle half of onion and seasoned salt over potatoes; top with half of bacon and cheese. Repeat layers. Sprinkle water over top.

2 Cover; cook on LOW 6 hours or on HIGH 3½ hours or until potatoes and onion are tender. Stir gently to mix; serve warm.

Four Fruit Oatmeal

Makes 4 servings

4¼ cups water

1 cup steel-cut oats

⅓ cup golden raisins

⅓ cup dried cranberries

⅓ cup dried cherries

2 tablespoons honey

1 teaspoon vanilla

¼ teaspoon salt

1 cup fresh sliced strawberries

Combine water, oats, raisins, cranberries, cherries, honey, vanilla and salt in **CROCK-POT®** slow cooker; stir to blend. Cover; cook on LOW 7 to 7½ hours. Top each serving evenly with strawberries.

Maple, Bacon and Raspberry Pancake

Makes 8 servings

5 slices bacon

2 cups pancake mix

1 cup water

½ cup maple syrup, plus additional for serving

1 cup fresh raspberries, plus additional for garnish

3 tablespoons chopped pecans, toasted*

*To toast pecans, spread in single layer in heavy skillet. Cook and stir over medium heat 1 to 2 minutes or until nuts are lightly browned.

1 Heat large skillet over medium heat. Add bacon; cook and stir until crisp. Remove to paper towel-lined plate using slotted spoon; crumble.

2 Brush inside of 5-quart **CROCK-POT**® slow cooker with 1 to 2 tablespoons drippings from skillet. Combine pancake mix, water and ½ cup maple syrup in large bowl; stir to blend. Pour half of batter into **CROCK-POT**® slow cooker; top with ½ cup raspberries, half of bacon and half of pecans. Pour remaining half of batter over top; sprinkle with remaining ½ cup raspberries, bacon and pecans.

3 Cover; cook on HIGH 1½ to 2 hours or until pancake has risen and is cooked through. Turn off heat. Let stand, uncovered, 10 to 15 minutes. Remove pancake from **CROCK-POT**® slow cooker; cut into eight pieces. Serve with additional maple syrup and raspberries.

Chocolate-Stuffed
Slow Cooker French Toast

Makes 6 servings

1 tablespoon butter, softened

6 slices (¾-inch-thick) day-old challah*

½ cup semisweet chocolate chips

6 eggs

3 cups half-and-half

⅔ cup granulated sugar

1 teaspoon vanilla

¼ teaspoon salt

Powdered sugar

Fresh fruit (optional)

*Challah is usually braided. If you use brioche or another rich egg bread, slice bread to fit baking dish.

1 Grease 2½-quart baking dish that fits inside of **CROCK-POT**® slow cooker with butter. Arrange 2 bread slices in bottom of dish. Sprinkle with ¼ cup chocolate chips. Add 2 bread slices. Sprinkle with remaining ¼ cup chocolate chips. Top with remaining 2 bread slices.

2 Beat eggs in large bowl. Stir in half-and-half, granulated sugar, vanilla and salt. Pour egg mixture over bread layers. Press bread into liquid. Set aside 10 minutes or until liquid is absorbed. Cover dish with buttered foil, buttered side down.

3 Pour 1 inch hot water into **CROCK-POT**® slow cooker. Add baking dish. Cover; cook on HIGH 3 hours or until toothpick inserted into center comes out clean. Remove dish and let stand 10 minutes. Sprinkle with powdered sugar. Serve with fresh fruit, if desired.

 Tip Any oven-safe casserole or baking dish is safe to use in your **CROCK-POT**® slow cooker. Place directly inside the stoneware and follow the recipe directions.

Apple-Cinnamon Breakfast Risotto

Makes 6 servings

¼ cup (½ stick) butter

4 medium Granny Smith apples (about 1½ pounds), peeled, cored and diced into ½-inch cubes

1½ teaspoons ground cinnamon

¼ teaspoon ground allspice

¼ teaspoon salt

1½ cups uncooked Arborio rice

½ cup packed dark brown sugar

4 cups unfiltered apple juice, at room temperature*

1 teaspoon vanilla

Optional toppings: dried cranberries, sliced almonds and/or milk

*If unfiltered apple juice is unavailable, use any apple juice.

1 Coat inside of **CROCK-POT**® slow cooker with nonstick cooking spray. Melt butter in large skillet over medium-high heat. Add apples, cinnamon, allspice and salt; cook and stir 3 to 5 minutes or until apples begin to release juices. Remove to **CROCK-POT**® slow cooker.

2 Add rice; stir to coat. Sprinkle brown sugar evenly over top. Add apple juice and vanilla. Cover; cook on HIGH 1½ to 2 hours or until all liquid is absorbed. Ladle risotto into bowls; top as desired.

 Keep the lid on! The **CROCK-POT**® slow cooker can take as long as 30 minutes to regain heat lost when the cover is removed.

Taco Tuesday

Shredded Chicken Tacos

Makes 4 servings

2 pounds boneless, skinless chicken thighs

½ cup mango salsa, plus additional for serving

Lettuce (optional)

8 (6-inch) yellow corn tortillas, warmed

1 Coat inside of **CROCK-POT®** slow cooker with nonstick cooking spray. Add chicken and ½ cup salsa. Cover; cook on LOW 4 to 5 hours or on HIGH 2½ to 3 hours.

2 Remove chicken to large cutting board; shred with two forks. Add shredded chicken back into **CROCK-POT®** slow cooker. To serve, divide chicken and lettuce, if desired, evenly among tortillas. Serve with additional salsa.

Confetti Black Beans

Makes 6 servings

- 1 cup dried black beans, rinsed and sorted
- 1½ teaspoons olive oil
- 1 medium onion, chopped
- ¼ cup chopped red bell pepper
- ¼ cup chopped yellow bell pepper
- 1 jalapeño pepper, finely chopped*
- 1 large tomato, chopped
- ½ teaspoon salt
- ⅛ teaspoon black pepper
- 2 cloves garlic, minced
- 1 can (about 14 ounces) chicken broth
- 1 bay leaf
- Hot pepper sauce (optional)

*Jalapeño peppers can sting and irritate the skin, so wear rubber gloves when handling peppers and do not touch your eyes.

1 Place beans in large bowl and add enough cold water to cover by at least 2 inches. Soak 6 to 8 hours or overnight.** Drain beans; discard water.

2 Heat oil in large skillet over medium heat. Add onion, bell peppers and jalapeño pepper; cook and stir 5 minutes or until onion is tender. Add tomato, salt and black pepper; cook 5 minutes. Stir in garlic.

3 Place beans, broth and bay leaf in **CROCK-POT®** slow cooker. Add onion mixture. Cover; cook on LOW 7 to 8 hours or on HIGH 4½ to 5 hours. Remove and discard bay leaf. Serve with hot pepper sauce, if desired.

**To quick soak beans, place beans in large saucepan; cover with water. Bring to a boil over high heat. Boil 2 minutes. Remove from heat; let soak, covered, 1 hour.

Arroz con Queso

Makes 8 to 10 servings

1 can (about 14 ounces) crushed tomatoes, undrained

1 can (about 15 ounces) black beans, rinsed and drained

1½ cups uncooked converted long grain rice

1 onion, chopped

1 cup cottage cheese

1 can (4 ounces) chopped mild green chiles

2 tablespoons vegetable oil

3 teaspoons minced garlic

2 cups (8 ounces) shredded Monterey Jack cheese, divided

Sliced jalapeño pepper (optional)*

*Jalapeño peppers can sting and irritate the skin, so wear rubber gloves when handling peppers and do not touch your eyes.

Combine tomatoes, beans, rice, onion, cottage cheese, chiles, oil, garlic and 1 cup cheese in **CROCK-POT**® slow cooker; stir to blend. Cover; cook on LOW 6 to 9 hours or until liquid is absorbed. Sprinkle with remaining 1 cup cheese before serving. Garnish with jalapeño pepper.

Beefy Tortilla Pie
Makes 4 to 6 servings

· ·

2 teaspoons olive oil

1½ cups chopped onion

2 pounds ground beef

1 teaspoon salt

1 teaspoon ground cumin

1 teaspoon chili powder

2 cloves garlic, minced

1 can (15 ounces) tomato sauce

1 cup sliced pitted black olives

8 (6-inch) flour tortillas

3½ cups (14 ounces) shredded Cheddar cheese

Sour cream, salsa and/ or chopped green onions (optional)

· ·

1 Prepare foil handles.* Heat oil in large skillet over medium heat. Add onion; cook and stir 3 to 5 minutes or until tender. Add beef, salt, cumin, chili powder and garlic; cook and stir 6 to 8 minutes or until beef is browned. Drain fat. Stir in tomato sauce; cook until heated through. Stir in olives.

2 Lay 1 tortilla on foil strips. Spread with meat sauce and ½ cup cheese. Top with another tortilla, meat sauce and cheese. Repeat layers five times, ending with tortilla. Cover; cook on HIGH 1½ hours.

3 Lift pie out of **CROCK-POT®** slow cooker using foil handles; remove to large serving platter. Discard foil. Cut into wedges. Serve with sour cream, salsa and green onions, if desired.

*Prepare foil handles by tearing off one 18-inch long piece of foil; fold in half lengthwise. Fold in half lengthwise again to create 18X3-inch strip. Repeat 2 times. Crisscross foil strips in spoke design; place in **CROCK-POT®** slow cooker. Leave strips in during cooking so you can easily lift the cooked item out again when cooking is complete.

Pozole Rojo

Makes 8 servings

- 4 dried ancho chiles, stemmed and seeded
- 3 dried guajillo chiles, stemmed and seeded*
- 2 cups boiling water
- 2½ pounds boneless pork shoulder, trimmed and cut in half
- 3 teaspoons salt, divided
- 1 tablespoon vegetable oil
- 1 large onion, chopped
- 1½ tablespoons minced garlic
- 2 teaspoons ground cumin

- 2 teaspoons Mexican oregano**
- 4 cups chicken broth
- 2 cans (30 ounces *each*) white hominy, rinsed and drained
- Optional toppings: sliced radishes, lime wedges, sliced romaine lettuce, chopped onion, tortilla chips and/or diced avocado

*Guajillo chiles can be found in the ethnic section of large supermarkets.

**Mexican oregano has a stronger flavor than regular oregano. It can be found in the spices and seasonings section of most large supermarkets.

1 Place ancho and guajillo chiles in medium bowl; pour boiling water over top. Weigh down chiles with small plate or bowl; soak 30 minutes.

2 Meanwhile, season pork with 1 teaspoon salt. Heat oil in large skillet over medium-high heat. Add pork; cook 8 to 10 minutes or until browned on all sides. Remove to **CROCK-POT**® slow cooker.

3 Heat same skillet over medium heat. Add onion; cook 6 minutes or until softened. Add garlic, cumin, oregano and remaining 2 teaspoons salt; cook and stir 1 minute. Stir in broth; bring to a simmer, scraping up any browned bits from bottom of skillet. Pour over pork in **CROCK-POT**® slow cooker.

4 Place softened chiles and soaking liquid in food processor or blender; process until smooth. Pour through fine-mesh sieve into medium bowl, pressing with spoon to extract liquid. Discard solids. Stir mixture into **CROCK-POT**® slow cooker.

5 Cover; cook on LOW 5 hours. Stir in hominy. Cover; cook on LOW 1 hour. Turn off heat. Let stand 10 to 15 minutes. Skim off fat and discard. Remove pork to large cutting board; shred with two forks. Ladle hominy mixture into bowls; top each serving with pork and desired toppings.

Nacho Dip

Makes 10 cups

1 tablespoon vegetable oil

1 onion, chopped

2 pounds ground beef

2 cans (about 15 ounces *each*) black beans, rinsed and drained

1 can (28 ounces) diced tomatoes

1 can (about 15 ounces) refried beans

1 can (about 15 ounces) cream-style corn

3 cloves garlic, minced

1 package (1¼ ounces) taco seasoning mix

Tortilla chips

Queso blanco

1 Heat oil in large skillet over medium-high heat. Add onion; cook 2 to 3 minutes or until translucent. Add beef; brown 6 to 8 minutes, stirring to break up meat. Drain fat.

2 Stir beef mixture, black beans, tomatoes, refried beans, corn, garlic and taco seasoning mix into **CROCK-POT®** slow cooker. Cover; cook on LOW 5 to 6 hours or on HIGH 2½ to 3 hours. Serve on tortilla chips. Sprinkle with queso blanco.

Mole Chili

Makes 4 to 6 servings

2 corn tortillas, each cut into 4 wedges

1½ pounds boneless beef chuck roast, cut into 1-inch pieces

¾ teaspoon salt

½ teaspoon black pepper

3 tablespoons olive oil, divided

2 medium onions, chopped

5 cloves garlic, minced

1 cup beef broth

1 can (about 14 ounces) fire-roasted diced tomatoes

2 tablespoons chili powder

1 tablespoon ground ancho chile

1 teaspoon ground cumin

1 teaspoon dried oregano

¾ teaspoon ground cinnamon

1 can (about 15 ounces) red kidney beans, rinsed and drained

2 ounces semisweet chocolate, chopped

Queso fresco and chopped fresh cilantro (optional)

1 Coat inside of **CROCK-POT®** slow cooker with nonstick cooking spray. Place tortillas in food processor or blender; process to fine crumbs. Set aside.

2 Season beef with salt and pepper. Heat 1 tablespoon oil in large skillet over medium-high heat. Add half of beef to skillet; cook 4 minutes or until browned. Remove to **CROCK-POT®** slow cooker. Repeat with remaining beef and 1 tablespoon oil.

3 Heat remaining 1 tablespoon oil in skillet. Add onions and garlic; cook 2 minutes or until beginning to soften. Pour broth into skillet, scraping up any browned bits from bottom of skillet. Remove to **CROCK-POT®** slow cooker. Stir in reserved tortilla crumbs, tomatoes, chili powder, ancho chile, cumin, oregano and cinnamon.

4 Cover; cook on LOW 8 to 8½ hours or on HIGH 4 to 4½ hours. Stir in beans. Cover; cook on LOW 30 minutes. Turn off heat. Stir in chocolate until melted. Top with queso fresco and cilantro, if desired.

Pulled Pork Enchiladas

Makes 12 servings

1 can (about 14 ounces) chicken broth

1 medium onion, chopped

2 cloves garlic, minced

2 teaspoons ground cumin

1 teaspoon ground cinnamon

½ teaspoon black pepper

1 boneless pork shoulder roast (3 pounds), trimmed*

2 cans (10 ounces *each*) enchilada sauce, divided

1 cup salsa

1 cup (4 ounces) shredded Mexican cheese blend, divided

1 can (4 ounces) diced mild green chiles

12 (6-inch) flour tortillas

Sour cream (optional)

Fresh cilantro sprigs (optional)

*Unless you have a 5-, 6- or 7-quart CROCK-POT® slow cooker, cut any roast larger than 2½ pounds so it cooks completely.

1 Combine broth, onion and garlic in **CROCK-POT®** slow cooker. Combine cumin, cinnamon and black pepper in small bowl; rub evenly onto pork. Place in **CROCK-POT®** slow cooker, seasoned side up. Cover; cook on LOW 12 to 14 hours or on HIGH 6 to 7 hours or until pork is fork-tender.

2 Remove pork to large cutting board; shred with two forks. Measure 3 cups; reserve remaining pork for another use.

3 Preheat oven to 375°F. Combine 3 cups pork, ½ can enchilada sauce, salsa and ¾ cup cheese in large bowl. Spread ½ can enchilada sauce and diced green chiles in 13×9-inch baking dish. Spread ¼ cup pork mixture on each tortilla. Roll up and place seam side down in baking dish. Spread remaining 1 can enchilada sauce over tortillas.

4 Bake 20 minutes. Top with remaining ¼ cup cheese; bake 10 minutes or until cheese is melted. Serve with sour cream and cilantro, if desired.

Chipotle Chicken Stew

Makes 6 servings

1 pound boneless, skinless chicken thighs, cubed

1 can (about 15 ounces) navy beans, rinsed and drained

1 can (about 15 ounces) black beans, rinsed and drained

1 can (about 14 ounces) crushed tomatoes, undrained

1½ cups chicken broth

½ cup orange juice

1 medium onion, diced

1 canned chipotle pepper in adobo sauce, minced

1 teaspoon salt

1 teaspoon ground cumin

1 bay leaf

Fresh cilantro sprigs (optional)

1 Combine chicken, beans, tomatoes, broth, orange juice, onion, chipotle pepper, salt, cumin and bay leaf in **CROCK-POT®** slow cooker.

2 Cover; cook on LOW 7 to 8 hours or on HIGH 3½ to 4 hours. Remove and discard bay leaf. Garnish with cilantro.

Carnitas in Bell Peppers

Makes 8 servings

½ cup chicken broth

1 teaspoon salt

1 teaspoon minced garlic

½ teaspoon ground cumin

½ teaspoon dried oregano

½ teaspoon chili powder

½ teaspoon black pepper

2 bay leaves

2 pounds boneless pork roast

8 bell peppers (any color), halved

Optional toppings: guacamole, salsa and/or shredded cheese

1 Coat inside of **CROCK-POT®** slow cooker with nonstick cooking spray; add broth.

2 Combine salt, garlic, cumin, oregano, chili powder, black pepper and bay leaves in small bowl; stir to blend. Rub salt mixture over pork; place in **CROCK-POT®** slow cooker.

3 Cover; cook on HIGH 3½ hours. Remove pork to large cutting board; shred with two forks. Divide shredded pork evenly between peppers. Top as desired.

Fiery Southwestern Enchiladas

Makes 8 servings

Steak Filling:

- **2** pounds tri-tip steak, cut into large cubes
- **1** cup water
- **½** cup tequila
- **5** cloves garlic, minced
- **1** serrano pepper, diced*
- **1** jalapeño pepper, diced*
  Kosher salt and black pepper

Enchilada Sauce:

- **5** cans (7 ounces *each*) tomatillo sauce
- **1½** cups tomato sauce
- **1** pound Monterey Jack cheese, shredded and divided

- **3** cans (about 15 ounces *each*) black beans, rinsed and drained
- **1** can (8 ounces) corn, drained
- **16** flour tortillas
- **1** can (7 ounces) diced mild green chiles
- **½** cup sour cream (optional)
- **1** cup chopped fresh tomato
- **¼** cup fresh chives, chopped

*Serrano and jalapeño peppers can sting and irritate the skin, so wear rubber gloves when handling peppers and do not touch your eyes.

1 Combine steak, water, tequila, garlic, serrano and jalapeño peppers in **CROCK-POT®** slow cooker. Season with salt and black pepper. Cover; cook on LOW 10 to 12 hours or until very tender. Remove steak to cutting board; shred with two forks. Refrigerate until ready to use.

2 Preheat oven to 375°F. Spray 13×9-inch baking pan with nonstick cooking spray. Combine tomatillo and tomato sauces in large saucepan over medium heat; cook and stir until heated through. Stir in ¼ cup cheese.

3 Heat beans and corn in another large saucepan. Fill tortillas evenly with sauce, beans, corn, 3 tablespoons cheese, steak and diced green chiles, reserving ¼ cup *each* cheese and sauce for topping. Roll tortillas; arrange in prepared baking pan. Top with reserved sauce and cheese.

4 Cover prepared baking pan with foil; bake 15 minutes. Top with sour cream, if desired, tomato and chives. Serve immediately.

Sweet and Spicy Pork Picadillo
Makes 4 servings

1 tablespoon olive oil

1 yellow onion, cut into ¼-inch pieces

2 cloves garlic, minced

1 pound boneless pork country-style ribs, trimmed and cut into 1-inch cubes

1 can (about 14 ounces) diced tomatoes

3 tablespoons cider vinegar

2 canned chipotle peppers in adobo sauce, chopped*

½ cup raisins

½ teaspoon ground cumin

½ teaspoon ground cinnamon

Hot cooked rice (optional)

Black beans (optional)

*You may substitute dried chipotle peppers, soaked in warm water about 20 minutes to soften before chopping.

1 Heat oil in large skillet over medium-low heat. Add onion and garlic; cook and stir 4 minutes. Add pork; cook and stir 5 to 7 minutes or until browned. Remove to **CROCK-POT**® slow cooker.

2 Add tomatoes, vinegar, chipotle peppers, raisins, cumin and cinnamon to **CROCK-POT**® slow cooker; stir to blend. Cover; cook on LOW 5 hours or on HIGH 3 hours. Remove pork to large cutting board; shred with two forks. Return pork to **CROCK-POT**® slow cooker; stir to blend. Cover; cook on HIGH 30 minutes. Serve with rice and beans, if desired.

Mexican Chicken and Black Bean Soup

Makes 4 servings

- 4 bone-in chicken thighs, skin removed
- 1 cup finely chopped onion
- 1 can (about 14 ounces) chicken broth
- 1 can (about 14 ounces) diced tomatoes with Mexican seasoning or diced tomatoes with mild green chiles
- 1 can (about 15 ounces) black beans, rinsed and drained

- 1 cup frozen corn
- 1 can (4 ounces) chopped mild green chiles
- 1 tablespoon chili powder
- 1 teaspoon salt
- 1 teaspoon ground cumin

  Optional toppings: sour cream, sliced avocado, shredded cheese, chopped fresh cilantro and/or fried tortilla strips

1 Coat inside of **CROCK-POT**® slow cooker with nonstick cooking spray. Combine chicken, onion, broth, tomatoes with chiles, beans, corn, chiles, chili powder, salt and cumin in **CROCK-POT**® slow cooker; stir to blend. Cover; cook on HIGH 3 to 4 hours or until chicken is cooked through.

2 Remove chicken to large cutting board. Debone and chop chicken. Return to **CROCK-POT**® slow cooker; stir well. Serve in bowls. Top as desired.

Chile Rellenos

Makes 6 servings

6 whole poblano peppers

2½ cups (10 ounces) grated Chihuahua cheese or queso fresco, divided

½ cup plus 2 tablespoons salsa verde, divided

¼ cup plus 2 tablespoons fresh cilantro, divided

1 (1-inch) piece fresh serrano pepper

1 large clove garlic

1 can (12 ounces) evaporated milk

2 tablespoons all-purpose flour

2 eggs

⅔ cup sour cream

1 Coat inside of **CROCK-POT**® slow cooker with nonstick cooking spray. Place poblano peppers under broiler, about 4 inches from heat. Broil just until skins blister. Let cool slightly in large paper bag. Peel poblano peppers when cool enough to handle. Cut down one side of each poblano pepper; open flat to remove any seeds or membranes inside. Pat dry with paper towels.

2 Divide 1½ cups cheese evenly among poblano peppers; roll to enclose. Lay poblano peppers in single layer in bottom of **CROCK-POT**® slow cooker.

3 Combine ½ cup salsa verde, ¼ cup cilantro, serrano pepper and garlic in food processor or blender; pulse to blend. Add evaporated milk, flour and eggs; process until smooth. Pour salsa mixture over poblano peppers; top with remaining 1 cup cheese. Cover; cook on LOW 3 hours.

4 Meanwhile, combine sour cream and remaining 2 tablespoons salsa verde in small bowl; stir to blend. Refrigerate sour cream mixture until ready to serve.

5 If desired, remove poblano peppers from **CROCK-POT**® slow cooker onto large baking sheet. Broil 3 to 5 minutes. Garnish with sour cream mixture and remaining 2 tablespoons cilantro.

Black Bean and Mushroom Chilaquiles

Makes 6 servings

- 2 tablespoons olive oil
- 1 medium onion, chopped
- 1 medium green bell pepper, chopped
- 1 jalapeño or serrano pepper, seeded and minced*
- 2 cans (about 15 ounces *each*) black beans, rinsed and drained
- 1 can (about 14 ounces) diced tomatoes
- 10 ounces white mushrooms, cut into quarters
- 1½ teaspoons ground cumin
- 1½ teaspoons dried oregano
- 1 cup (4 ounces) shredded sharp white Cheddar cheese, plus additional for garnish
- 6 cups baked tortilla chips

*Jalapeño and serrano peppers can sting and irritate the skin, so wear rubber gloves when handling peppers and do not touch your eyes.

1 Heat oil in medium skillet over medium heat. Add onion, bell pepper and jalapeño pepper; cook and stir 5 minutes or until onion is softened. Remove to **CROCK-POT**® slow cooker. Add beans, tomatoes, mushrooms, cumin and oregano. Cover; cook on LOW 6 hours or on HIGH 3 hours.

2 Sprinkle 1 cup cheese over beans and mushrooms. Cover; cook on HIGH 15 minutes or until cheese is melted. Stir to blend.

3 For each serving, coarsely crush 1 cup tortilla chips into individual serving bowls. Top with black bean mixture. Garnish with additional cheese.

Pizza and Pasta

Pepperoni Pizza Monkey Bread

Makes 12 servings

1 package (about 3 ounces) pepperoni, divided

1 teaspoon minced garlic

¼ teaspoon red pepper flakes

1 package (about 16 ounces) refrigerated biscuits, each biscuit cut into 6 pieces

1 can (15 ounces) pizza sauce

1 small green bell pepper, chopped

1 small yellow bell pepper, chopped

1 package (8 ounces) shredded mozzarella cheese

1 Coat inside of **CROCK-POT®** slow cooker with nonstick cooking spray. Prepare foil handles.* Spray foil handles with cooking spray.

2 Chop half of pepperoni slices. Combine chopped pepperoni, garlic and red pepper flakes in medium bowl. Roll each biscuit piece into pepperoni mixture; place in **CROCK-POT®** slow cooker. Pour half of pizza sauce over dough. Reserve remaining pizza sauce. Top sauce with bell peppers, cheese and remaining half of pepperoni slices.

3 Cover; cook on LOW 3 hours. Turn off heat. Let pizza stand 10 to 15 minutes. Remove from **CROCK-POT®** slow cooker using foil handles. Serve with remaining pizza sauce for dipping.

*Prepare foil handles by tearing off one 18-inch long piece of foil; fold in half lengthwise. Fold in half lengthwise again to create 18X3-inch strip. Repeat 2 times. Crisscross foil strips in spoke design; place in **CROCK-POT®** slow cooker. Leave strips in during cooking so you can easily lift the cooked item out again when cooking is complete.

Pasta Fagioli Soup

Makes 5 to 6 servings

2 cans (about 14 ounces *each*) vegetable broth

1 can (about 15 ounces) Great Northern beans, rinsed and drained

1 can (about 14 ounces) diced tomatoes

2 zucchini, quartered lengthwise and sliced

1½ teaspoons minced garlic

½ teaspoon dried basil

½ teaspoon dried oregano

½ cup uncooked ditalini, tubetti or small shell pasta

½ cup garlic-seasoned croutons

½ cup grated Asiago or Romano cheese

3 tablespoons chopped fresh basil or Italian parsley (optional)

1 Combine broth, beans, tomatoes, zucchini, garlic, dried basil and oregano in **CROCK-POT®** slow cooker; stir to blend. Cover; cook on LOW 3 to 4 hours.

2 Stir in pasta. Cover; cook on LOW 1 hour or until pasta is tender. Serve soup with croutons and cheese. Garnish with fresh basil.

 Tip Only small pasta varieties should be used in this recipe. The low heat of a **CROCK-POT®** slow cooker will not allow larger pasta shapes to cook completely in 1 hour.

Italian Hillside Garden Soup

Makes 6 servings

· ·

1 tablespoon olive oil

1 cup chopped green bell pepper

1 cup chopped onion

½ cup sliced celery

1 can (about 14 ounces) diced tomatoes with basil, garlic and oregano

1 can (about 15 ounces) navy beans, rinsed and drained

1 medium zucchini, chopped

1 cup frozen cut green beans

2 cans (about 14 ounces *each*) chicken broth

¼ teaspoon garlic powder

1 package (9 ounces) refrigerated sausage- or cheese-filled tortellini pasta

3 tablespoons chopped fresh basil

Grated Asiago or Parmesan cheese (optional)

· ·

1 Heat oil in large skillet over medium-high heat. Add bell pepper, onion and celery; cook and stir 4 minutes or until onion is translucent. Remove to **CROCK-POT®** slow cooker.

2 Add tomatoes, navy beans, zucchini, green beans, broth and garlic powder; stir to blend. Cover; cook on LOW 7 hours or on HIGH 3½ hours.

3 Add tortellini. Cover; cook on HIGH 20 to 25 minutes or until pasta is tender. Stir in basil. Garnish with cheese.

 Tip Cooking times are guidelines. **CROCK-POT®** slow cookers, just like ovens, cook differently depending on a variety of factors, including capacity and altitude.

Spinach and Ricotta Stuffed Shells
Makes 6 servings

18 uncooked jumbo pasta shells (about half of a 12-ounce package)

1 package (15 ounces) ricotta cheese

7 ounces frozen chopped spinach, thawed and squeezed dry

½ cup grated Parmesan cheese

1 egg, lightly beaten

1 clove garlic, minced

½ teaspoon salt

1 jar (24 to 26 ounces) marinara sauce

½ cup (2 ounces) shredded mozzarella cheese

1 teaspoon olive oil

1 Cook pasta shells according to package directions until almost tender. Drain well. Combine ricotta cheese, spinach, Parmesan cheese, egg, garlic and salt in medium bowl.

2 Pour ¼ cup marinara sauce in bottom of **CROCK-POT®** slow cooker. Spoon 2 to 3 tablespoons ricotta mixture into 1 pasta shell and place in bottom of **CROCK-POT®** slow cooker. Repeat with enough additional shells to cover bottom of **CROCK-POT®** slow cooker. Top with another ¼ cup marinara sauce. Repeat with remaining pasta shells and filling.

3 Top with remaining marinara sauce and sprinkle with mozzarella cheese. Drizzle with oil. Cover; cook on HIGH 3 to 4 hours or until mozzarella cheese is melted and sauce is hot and bubbly.

Garden Pasta

Makes 4 to 6 servings

1 jar (24 to 26 ounces) puttanesca or spicy tomato basil pasta sauce

1 can (about 14 ounces) stewed tomatoes

1 small head broccoli florets (about 2 cups)

1 small zucchini, chopped (about 2 cups)

1 small yellow squash, chopped (about 2 cups)

½ cup water

1 package (12 ounces) uncooked bowtie pasta

1 teaspoon salt

½ cup crumbled feta cheese

¼ cup chopped fresh basil

1 Coat inside of **CROCK-POT®** slow cooker with nonstick cooking spray. Combine pasta sauce, tomatoes, broccoli, zucchini, squash, water and pasta in **CROCK-POT®** slow cooker; stir to blend.

2 Cover; cook on LOW 3½ to 4½ hours or on HIGH 2 to 2½ hours, stirring halfway through cooking time. Season with salt. Spoon into shallow bowls; top with cheese and basil.

Creamy Chicken and Spinach Lasagna

Makes 4 servings

1¼ cups (5 ounces) shredded Swiss or mozzarella cheese, divided

1 cup ricotta cheese

1 teaspoon dried oregano

¼ teaspoon red pepper flakes, plus additional for garnish

1 container (10 ounces) refrigerated Alfredo pasta sauce

⅓ cup water

4 uncooked no-boil lasagna noodles

1 package (10 ounces) frozen chopped spinach, thawed and squeezed dry

1½ cups cooked diced chicken

¼ cup grated Parmesan cheese

1 Combine 1 cup Swiss cheese, ricotta cheese, oregano and ¼ teaspoon red pepper flakes in small bowl; set aside. Combine Alfredo sauce and water in medium bowl; stir to blend. Set aside.

2 Coat inside of **CROCK-POT**® slow cooker with nonstick cooking spray. Break 2 lasagna noodles in half and place on bottom. Spread half of ricotta mixture over noodles. Top with half of spinach. Arrange half of chicken and half of Parmesan over spinach. Pour half of Alfredo mixture over top. Repeat layers, beginning with noodles and ending with Alfredo mixture. Cover; cook on LOW 3 hours.

3 Turn off heat. Sprinkle remaining ¼ cup Swiss cheese on top. Cover and let stand 5 minutes or until cheese is melted. To serve, cut into squares or wedges. Garnish with additional red pepper flakes.

Pizza Fondue

Makes 20 to 25 servings

½ pound bulk Italian sausage

1 cup chopped onion

2 jars (24 to 26 ounces *each*) meatless pasta sauce

4 ounces thinly sliced ham, finely chopped

1 package (3 ounces) sliced pepperoni, finely chopped

¼ teaspoon red pepper flakes

1 pound mozzarella cheese, cut into ¾-inch cubes

1 loaf Italian or French bread, cut into 1-inch cubes

1 Brown sausage and onion in large skillet over medium-high heat 6 to 8 minutes, stirring to break up meat. Remove to **CROCK-POT®** slow cooker using slotted spoon.

2 Stir in pasta sauce, ham, pepperoni and red pepper flakes. Cover; cook on LOW 3 to 4 hours. Serve with cheese and bread cubes.

Hearty Vegetarian Mac and Cheese

Makes 6 servings

- 1 can (about 14 ounces) stewed tomatoes, undrained
- 1½ cups prepared Alfredo sauce
- 1½ cups (6 ounces) shredded mozzarella cheese, divided
- 8 ounces whole grain pasta (medium shells or penne shape), cooked and drained

- 7 ounces Italian-flavored vegetarian sausage links, ¼-inch slices
- ¾ cup fresh basil leaves, thinly sliced and divided
- ½ cup vegetable broth
- ½ teaspoon salt
- 2 tablespoons grated Parmesan cheese

1 Coat inside of **CROCK-POT®** slow cooker with nonstick cooking spray. Add tomatoes, Alfredo sauce, 1 cup mozzarella cheese, pasta, sausage, ½ cup basil, broth and salt to **CROCK-POT®** slow cooker; stir to blend. Top with remaining ½ cup mozzarella cheese and Parmesan cheese.

2 Cover; cook on LOW 3½ hours or on HIGH 2 hours. Top with remaining ¼ cup basil.

Pepperoni Pizza Dip

Makes 1⅓ cups

1 jar (about 14 ounces) pizza sauce

⅓ cup chopped pepperoni

½ can (about 2¼ ounces) sliced black olives, drained

1 teaspoon dried oregano

¼ cup (1 ounce) shredded mozzarella cheese

½ package (about 1½ ounces) cream cheese, softened

1 tablespoon olive oil

Breadsticks

1 Combine pizza sauce, pepperoni, olives and oregano in medium saucepan; stir to blend. Bring to a boil over medium-high heat, stirring frequently. Reduce heat to low. Stir in mozzarella cheese and cream cheese until melted. Remove from heat and stir in oil.

2 Coat inside of **CROCK-POT**® "No Dial" food warmer slow cooker with nonstick cooking spray. Fill with dip to keep warm. Serve with breadsticks.

Chicken Scaloppine in Alfredo Sauce

Makes 6 servings

2 tablespoons all-purpose flour

¼ teaspoon salt

¼ teaspoon black pepper

6 boneless, skinless chicken tenderloins (about 1 pound), cut lengthwise in half

1 tablespoon butter

1 tablespoon olive oil

1 cup Alfredo pasta sauce

1 package (12 ounces) uncooked spinach noodles

1 Place flour, salt and pepper in large bowl; stir to combine. Add chicken; toss to coat. Heat butter and oil in large skillet over medium-high heat. Add chicken; cook 3 minutes per side or until browned. Remove chicken to **CROCK-POT**® slow cooker.

2 Add pasta sauce to **CROCK-POT**® slow cooker. Cover; cook on LOW 1 to 1½ hours.

3 Meanwhile, cook noodles according to package directions. Drain; place in large shallow bowl. Spoon chicken and sauce over noodles.

Pizza-Style Mostaccioli

Makes 4 servings

1 jar (24 to 26 ounces) marinara sauce or tomato-basil pasta sauce

½ cup water

2 cups (6 ounces) uncooked mostaccioli pasta

1 package (8 ounces) sliced mushrooms

1 small yellow or green bell pepper, finely diced

½ cup (1 ounce) sliced pepperoni, halved

1 teaspoon dried oregano

¼ teaspoon red pepper flakes

1 cup (4 ounces) shredded pizza cheese blend or Italian cheese blend

Chopped fresh oregano (optional)

Garlic bread (optional)

1 Coat inside of **CROCK-POT®** slow cooker with nonstick cooking spray. Combine marinara sauce and water in **CROCK-POT®** slow cooker. Stir in pasta, mushrooms, bell pepper, pepperoni, dried oregano and red pepper flakes; mix well. Cover; cook on LOW 2 hours or on HIGH 1 hour.

2 Stir well. Cover; cook on LOW 1½ to 2 hours or on HIGH 45 minutes to 1 hour or until pasta and vegetables are tender. Spoon into shallow bowls. Top with cheese and garnish with fresh oregano. Serve with bread, if desired.

 Tip Stirring the pasta halfway through the cooking time prevents it from becoming overcooked on the bottom of the **CROCK-POT®** slow cooker.

Chicken Parmesan with Eggplant

Makes 6 to 8 servings

- 6 boneless, skinless chicken breasts
- 2 eggs
- 2 teaspoons salt
- 2 teaspoons black pepper
- 2 cups seasoned dry bread crumbs
- ½ cup olive oil
- ½ cup (1 stick) butter
- 2 small eggplants, cut into ¾-inch-thick slices
- 1½ cups grated Parmesan cheese
- 2¼ cups tomato-basil pasta sauce
- 1 pound (16 ounces) shredded mozzarella cheese
- Fresh basil sprigs (optional)

1 Slice chicken breasts in half lengthwise. Cut each half lengthwise again to get four ¾-inch slices.

2 Combine eggs, salt and pepper in medium bowl; whisk to blend. Place bread crumbs in separate medium bowl. Dip chicken in egg mixture; turn to coat. Then coat chicken with bread crumbs, covering both sides evenly.

3 Heat oil and butter in large skillet over medium heat. Add breaded chicken; cook 6 to 8 minutes until browned on both sides. Remove to paper towel-lined plate to drain excess oil.

4 Layer half of eggplant, ¾ cup Parmesan cheese and 1 cup pasta sauce in bottom of **CROCK-POT®** slow cooker. Top with half of chicken, remaining half of eggplant, remaining ¾ cup Parmesan cheese and ¼ cup pasta sauce. Arrange remaining half of chicken on sauce; top with remaining 1 cup pasta sauce and mozzarella cheese. Cover; cook on LOW 6 hours or on HIGH 2 to 4 hours. Garnish with fresh basil.

Pizza Soup

Makes 4 servings

- **2** cans (about 14 ounces *each*) stewed tomatoes with Italian seasonings, undrained
- **2** cups beef broth
- **1** cup sliced mushrooms
- **1** small onion, chopped
- **1** tablespoon tomato paste
- **¼** teaspoon salt
- **¼** teaspoon black pepper
- **½** pound turkey Italian sausage, casings removed

  Shredded mozzarella cheese

1 Combine tomatoes, broth, mushrooms, onion, tomato paste, salt and pepper in **CROCK-POT®** slow cooker; stir to blend.

2 Shape sausage into marble-size balls; stir into soup mixture. Cover; cook on LOW 6 to 7 hours. Top with cheese.

Easy Parmesan Chicken

Makes 4 servings

- 8 ounces mushrooms, sliced
- 1 medium onion, cut into thin wedges
- 1 tablespoon olive oil
- 4 boneless, skinless chicken breasts
- 1 jar (24 to 26 ounces) pasta sauce
- ½ teaspoon dried basil
- ¼ teaspoon dried oregano
- 1 bay leaf
- ½ cup (2 ounces) shredded mozzarella cheese
- ¼ cup grated Parmesan cheese
- Hot cooked spaghetti
- Chopped fresh basil (optional)

1 Place mushrooms and onion in **CROCK-POT**® slow cooker.

2 Heat oil in large skillet over medium-high heat. Add chicken; cook 5 to 6 minutes on each side or until browned. Place chicken in **CROCK-POT**® slow cooker. Pour pasta sauce over chicken; add dried basil, oregano and bay leaf. Cover; cook on LOW 6 to 7 hours or on HIGH 3 to 4 hours. Remove and discard bay leaf.

3 Sprinkle chicken with cheeses. Cook, uncovered, on LOW 10 minutes or until cheeses are melted. Serve over spaghetti and garnish with fresh basil.

 Dairy products should be added at the end of the cooking time, because they will curdle if cooked in the **CROCK-POT**® slow cooker for a long time.

Scallops in Fresh Tomato and Herb Sauce

Makes 4 servings

2 tablespoons vegetable oil

1 medium red onion, peeled and diced

1 clove garlic, minced

3½ cups fresh tomatoes, peeled*

1 can (12 ounces) tomato pureé

1 can (6 ounces) tomato paste

¼ cup dry red wine

2 tablespoons chopped fresh Italian parsley

1 tablespoon chopped fresh oregano

¼ teaspoon black pepper

1½ pounds fresh scallops, cleaned and drained

Hot cooked pasta or rice (optional)

*To peel tomatoes, place one at a time in simmering water about 10 seconds. (Add 30 seconds if tomatoes are not fully ripened.) Immediately plunge into a bowl of cold water for another 10 seconds. Peel skin with a knife.

1 Heat oil in medium skillet over medium heat. Add onion and garlic; cook and stir 7 to 8 minutes or until onion is soft and translucent. Remove to **CROCK-POT®** slow cooker.

2 Add tomatoes, tomato purée, tomato paste, wine, parsley, oregano and pepper. Cover; cook on LOW 6 to 8 hours.

3 Turn **CROCK-POT®** slow cooker to HIGH. Add scallops. Cover; cook on HIGH 15 minutes or until scallops are cooked through. Serve over pasta, if desired.

Beefy Tortellini

Makes 6 servings

½ pound ground beef

1 jar (24 to 26 ounces) roasted tomato and garlic pasta sauce

1 package (12 ounces) uncooked three-cheese tortellini

8 ounces sliced button or exotic mushrooms, such as oyster, shiitake and cremini

½ cup water

½ teaspoon red pepper flakes (optional)

¾ cup grated Asiago or Romano cheese

Chopped fresh Italian parsley (optional)

1 Coat inside of **CROCK-POT®** slow cooker with nonstick cooking spray. Brown beef in large skillet over medium-high heat 6 to 8 minutes, stirring to break up meat. Remove to **CROCK-POT®** slow cooker using slotted spoon.

2 Stir pasta sauce, tortellini, mushrooms, water and red pepper flakes, if desired, into **CROCK-POT®** slow cooker. Cover; cook on LOW 2 hours or on HIGH 1 hour. Stir.

3 Cover; cook on LOW 2 to 2½ hours or on HIGH ½ to 1 hour. Serve in shallow bowls topped with cheese and parsley, if desired.

Meat Lovers

Mom's Brisket

Makes 4 servings

4 teaspoons paprika, divided

1 beef brisket (about 2 pounds), scored on both sides

Olive oil

2 cups water

1½ cups ketchup

2 large onions, diced

2 tablespoons horseradish

4 Yukon Gold potatoes, cut into 1-inch pieces

Kosher salt and black pepper

1 Rub 2 teaspoons paprika evenly over beef. Heat oil in large skillet over medium heat. Brown brisket on both sides. Remove to **CROCK-POT®** slow cooker.

2 Combine water, ketchup, onions and horseradish in small bowl; stir to blend. Add to **CROCK-POT®** slow cooker. Cover; cook on LOW 7 to 9 hours or on HIGH 3 to 5 hours.

3 Remove meat to large cutting board. Cool and cut in thin diagonal slices. (At this point, meat can be refrigerated overnight.)

4 Sprinkle potatoes with remaining 2 teaspoons paprika. Place in **CROCK-POT®** slow cooker. Place sliced meat on top of potatoes. Season with salt and pepper. Cover; cook on LOW 6 to 8 hours or on HIGH 3 to 4 hours.

Italian Meatball Hoagies

Makes 4 servings

½ pound ground beef

½ pound Italian sausage, casings removed

¼ cup seasoned dry bread crumbs

¼ cup grated Parmesan cheese, plus additional for topping

1 egg

1 tablespoon olive oil

1 cup pasta sauce

2 tablespoons tomato paste

¼ teaspoon red pepper flakes (optional)

4 (6-inch) hoagie rolls, split

1 Coat inside of **CROCK-POT®** slow cooker with nonstick cooking spray. Combine beef, sausage, bread crumbs, ¼ cup cheese and egg in large bowl; mix well. Shape to form 12 (1½-inch) meatballs.

2 Heat oil in large skillet over medium heat. Add meatballs; cook 6 to 8 minutes or until browned on all sides, turning occasionally. Remove meatballs to **CROCK-POT®** slow cooker using slotted spoon.

3 Combine pasta sauce, tomato paste and red pepper flakes, if desired, in medium bowl; stir to blend. Spoon over meatballs; toss gently.

4 Cover; cook on LOW 5 to 7 hours or on HIGH 2½ to 3 hours. Place meatballs in rolls. Spoon sauce over meatballs; top with additional cheese.

Classic Beef Stew

Makes 8 servings

2½ pounds cubed beef stew meat

¼ cup all-purpose flour

2 tablespoons olive oil, divided

3 cups beef broth

16 baby carrots

8 fingerling potatoes, halved crosswise

1 medium onion, chopped

1 ounce dried oyster mushrooms, chopped

2 teaspoons garlic powder

1 teaspoon dried basil

1 teaspoon dried oregano

½ teaspoon dried rosemary

½ teaspoon dried marjoram

½ teaspoon dried sage

½ teaspoon dried thyme

Salt and black pepper (optional)

Chopped fresh Italian parsley (optional)

1 Combine beef and flour in large resealable food storage bag; toss to coat. Heat 1 tablespoon oil in large skillet over medium-high heat. Add half of beef; cook and stir 4 minutes or until browned. Remove to **CROCK-POT**® slow cooker. Repeat with remaining oil and beef.

2 Add broth, carrots, potatoes, onion, mushrooms, garlic powder, basil, oregano, rosemary, marjoram, sage and thyme to **CROCK-POT**® slow cooker; stir to blend.

3 Cover; cook on LOW 10 to 12 hours or on HIGH 5 to 6 hours. Season with salt and pepper, if desired. Garnish with parsley.

Harvest Ham Supper

Makes 6 servings

· ·

6 medium carrots, halved and
   cut into 2-inch pieces

3 medium unpeeled sweet
   potatoes, quartered

1 to 1½ pounds boneless ham

½ cup maple syrup

Chopped fresh Italian parsley
   (optional)

· ·

1 Arrange carrots and potatoes in bottom of **CROCK-POT®** slow cooker. Place ham on top of vegetables. Pour maple syrup over ham and vegetables.

2 Cover; cook on LOW 6 to 8 hours. Garnish vegetables with parsley.

Hot and Juicy Reuben Sandwiches

Makes 4 servings

· ·

1 corned beef brisket, trimmed
   (about 1½ pounds)

2 cups sauerkraut, drained

½ cup beef broth

1 small onion, sliced

1 clove garlic, minced

¼ teaspoon caraway seeds

4 to 6 black peppercorns

8 slices pumpernickel or rye bread

4 slices Swiss cheese

Prepared mustard

· ·

1 Place corned beef, sauerkraut, broth, onion, garlic, caraway seeds and peppercorns in **CROCK-POT®** slow cooker. Cover; cook on LOW 7 to 9 hours.

2 Remove beef to large cutting board. Cut beef across grain into slices. Divide among 4 bread slices. Top each slice with drained sauerkraut mixture and 1 slice cheese. Spread mustard on remaining 4 bread slices; place on sandwiches.

Harvest Ham Supper

Cuban Pork Sandwiches

Makes 8 servings

1 pork loin roast (about 2 pounds)

½ cup orange juice

2 tablespoons lime juice

1 tablespoon minced garlic

1½ teaspoons salt

½ teaspoon red pepper flakes

2 tablespoons yellow mustard

8 crusty bread rolls, split in half (6 inches *each*)

8 slices Swiss cheese

8 thin ham slices

4 small dill pickles, thinly sliced lengthwise

Nonstick cooking spray

1 Coat inside of **CROCK-POT**® slow cooker with nonstick cooking spray. Add pork loin.

2 Combine orange juice, lime juice, garlic, salt and red pepper flakes in small bowl. Pour over pork. Cover; cook on LOW 7 to 8 hours or on HIGH 3½ to 4 hours. Remove pork to large cutting board. Cover loosely with foil; let stand 10 to 15 minutes before slicing.

3 To serve, spread mustard on both sides of rolls. Divide pork slices among roll bottoms. Top with Swiss cheese slice, ham slice and pickle slices; cover with top of roll.

4 Coat large skillet with nonstick cooking spray; heat over medium heat. Working in batches, arrange sandwiches in skillet. Cover with foil and top with dinner plate to press down sandwiches. (If necessary, weigh down with 2 to 3 cans to compress sandwiches lightly.) Heat about 8 minutes or until cheese is slightly melted.*

*Or use table top grill to compress and heat sandwiches.

Asian Barbecue Skewers

Makes 4 to 6 servings

2 pounds boneless, skinless chicken thighs

½ cup soy sauce

⅓ cup packed brown sugar

2 tablespoons dark sesame oil

3 cloves garlic, minced

½ cup thinly sliced green onions (optional)

1 tablespoon toasted sesame seeds (optional)*

*To toast sesame seeds, spread in small skillet. Shake skillet over medium-low heat 2 minutes or until seeds begin to pop and turn golden brown.

1 Cut each chicken thigh into four pieces, about 1½ inches thick. Thread chicken onto 7-inch-long wooden skewers, folding thinner pieces, if necessary. Place skewers into **CROCK-POT**® slow cooker, layering as flat as possible.

2 Combine soy sauce, brown sugar, oil and garlic in small bowl. Reserve ⅓ cup sauce; set aside. Pour remaining sauce over skewers. Cover; cook on LOW 2 hours. Turn skewers over. Cover; cook on LOW 1 hour.

3 Remove skewers to large serving platter. Discard cooking liquid. Pour reserved sauce over skewers. Sprinkle with green onions and sesame seeds, if desired.

Pulled Pork with Honey-Chipotle Barbecue Sauce

Makes 8 servings

· · · · · · · · · · · · · · · · · · · ·

1 tablespoon chili powder, divided

1 teaspoon chipotle chili powder, divided

1 teaspoon ground cumin, divided

1 teaspoon garlic powder, divided

1 teaspoon salt

1 bone-in pork shoulder (3½ pounds), trimmed*

1 can (15 ounces) tomato sauce

5 tablespoons honey, divided

*Unless you have a 5-, 6- or 7-quart CROCK-POT® slow cooker, cut any roast larger than 2½ pounds so it cooks completely.

· · · · · · · · · · · · · · · · · · · ·

1 Coat inside of **CROCK-POT®** slow cooker with nonstick cooking spray. Combine 1 teaspoon chili powder, ½ teaspoon chipotle chili powder, ½ teaspoon cumin, ½ teaspoon garlic powder and salt in small bowl. Rub pork with chili powder mixture. Place pork in **CROCK-POT®** slow cooker.

2 Combine tomato sauce, 4 tablespoons honey, remaining 2 teaspoons chili powder, ½ teaspoon chipotle chili powder, ½ teaspoon cumin and ½ teaspoon garlic powder in large bowl. Pour tomato mixture over pork in **CROCK-POT®** slow cooker. Cover; cook on LOW 8 hours.

3 Remove pork to large bowl; cover loosely with foil. Turn **CROCK-POT®** slow cooker to HIGH. Cover; cook on HIGH 30 minutes or until sauce is thickened. Stir in remaining 1 tablespoon honey. Turn off heat.

4 Remove bone from pork and discard. Shred pork using two forks. Stir shredded pork back into **CROCK-POT®** slow cooker to coat well with sauce.

Chicken Curry with Beer

Makes 4 servings

3 tablespoons vegetable oil

1 cut-up whole chicken (4 pounds)

Salt and black pepper

1 cup chicken broth

1 cup beer

1 cup tomato sauce

1 large onion, chopped

1 tablespoon minced ginger

2½ teaspoons curry powder

1 teaspoon salt

1 teaspoon garam masala

2 cloves garlic, minced

½ teaspoon chili powder

⅛ teaspoon ground red pepper

4 cups hot cooked basmati rice

1 Heat oil in large skillet over medium-high heat. Season chicken with salt and black pepper. Add chicken in batches; cook until browned on all sides.

2 Remove chicken to **CROCK-POT®** slow cooker. Add broth, beer, tomato sauce, onion, ginger, curry powder, 1 teaspoon salt, garam masala, garlic, chili powder and red pepper.

3 Cover; cook on LOW 8 hours. Serve chicken with sauce over rice.

Beef and Veal Meat Loaf

Makes 6 servings

1 tablespoon olive oil

1 small onion, chopped

½ red bell pepper, chopped

3 cloves garlic, minced

1 teaspoon dried oregano

1 pound ground beef

1 pound ground veal

1 egg

3 tablespoons tomato paste

1 teaspoon salt

½ teaspoon black pepper

1 Coat inside of **CROCK-POT®** slow cooker with nonstick cooking spray. Heat oil in large skillet over medium-high heat. Add onion, bell pepper, garlic and oregano; cook and stir 5 minutes or until vegetables are softened. Remove onion mixture to large bowl; cool 6 minutes.

2 Combine beef, veal, egg, tomato paste, salt and black pepper in large bowl with onion mixture; mix well. Form into 9×5-inch loaf; place in **CROCK-POT®** slow cooker.

3 Cover; cook on LOW 5 to 6 hours. Remove meat loaf to large cutting board; let stand 10 minutes before slicing.

Easy Salisbury Steak

Makes 4 servings

1½ **pounds ground beef**

1 **egg**

½ **cup plain dry bread crumbs**

1 **package (about 1 ounce) dry onion soup mix***

1 **can (10½ ounces) golden mushroom soup, undiluted**

*You may pulse onion soup mix in a small food processor or coffee grinder for a finer grind, if desired.

1 Coat inside of **CROCK-POT®** slow cooker with nonstick cooking spray. Combine beef, egg, bread crumbs and dry soup mix in large bowl. Form mixture evenly into four 1-inch-thick patties.

2 Heat large skillet over medium-high heat. Add patties; cook 2 minutes per side until lightly browned. Remove to **CROCK-POT®** slow cooker, in single layer. Pour mushroom soup evenly over patties. Cover; cook on LOW 3 to 3½ hours.

Maple-Dry Rubbed Ribs

Makes 4 servings

2 teaspoons chili powder, divided

1 teaspoon ground coriander

1 teaspoon garlic powder, divided

½ teaspoon salt

¼ teaspoon black pepper

3 to 3½ pounds pork baby back ribs, trimmed and cut in half

3 tablespoons maple syrup, divided

1 can (about 8 ounces) tomato sauce

¼ teaspoon ground cinnamon

¼ teaspoon ground ginger

1 Coat inside of **CROCK-POT®** slow cooker with nonstick cooking spray. Combine 1 teaspoon chili powder, coriander, ½ teaspoon garlic powder, salt and pepper in small bowl; stir to blend. Brush ribs with 1 tablespoon maple syrup; sprinkle with spice mixture. Remove ribs to **CROCK-POT®** slow cooker.

2 Combine tomato sauce, remaining 1 teaspoon chili powder, ½ teaspoon garlic powder, 2 tablespoons maple syrup, cinnamon and ginger in medium bowl; stir to blend. Pour tomato sauce mixture over ribs in **CROCK-POT®** slow cooker. Cover; cook on LOW 8 to 9 hours.

3 Remove ribs to large serving platter; cover with foil to keep warm. Turn **CROCK-POT®** slow cooker to HIGH. Cover; cook on HIGH 10 to 15 minutes or until sauce is thickened. Brush ribs with sauce and serve any remaining sauce on the side.

Boneless Pork Roast with Garlic

Makes 4 to 6 servings

1 boneless pork rib roast
  (2 to 2½ pounds)
  Salt and black pepper
3 tablespoons olive oil, divided
4 cloves garlic, minced

¼ cup chopped fresh rosemary
½ lemon, cut into ⅛- to ¼-inch slices
½ cup chicken broth
¼ cup dry white wine

1 Season pork with salt and pepper. Combine 2 tablespoons oil, garlic and rosemary in small bowl. Rub over pork. Roll and tie pork with kitchen string. Tuck lemon slices under string and into ends of roast.

2 Heat remaining 1 tablespoon oil in skillet over medium heat. Add pork; cook 6 to 8 minutes or until browned on all sides. Remove to **CROCK-POT®** slow cooker.

3 Return skillet to heat. Add broth and wine, scraping up any browned bits from bottom of skillet. Pour over pork in **CROCK-POT®** slow cooker. Cover; cook on LOW 8 to 9 hours or on HIGH 3 to 4 hours.

4 Remove roast to large cutting board. Cover loosely with foil; let stand 10 to 15 minutes before removing kitchen string and slicing. Pour pan juices over sliced pork to serve.

Beer Chicken

Makes 4 to 6 servings

2 tablespoons olive oil

1 cut-up whole chicken
(3 to 5 pounds)

10 unpeeled new potatoes, halved

1 can (12 ounces) beer

2 medium carrots, chopped
into 1-inch pieces

1 cup chopped celery

1 medium onion, chopped

1 tablespoon chopped fresh
rosemary

1 teaspoon salt

½ teaspoon black pepper

2 tablespoons water

2 tablespoons all-purpose flour

1 Heat oil in large skillet over medium heat. Add chicken; cook 5 to 7 minutes on each side or until browned. Remove to **CROCK-POT**® slow cooker.

2 Add potatoes, beer, carrots, celery, onion, rosemary, salt and pepper to **CROCK-POT**® slow cooker. Cover; cook on HIGH 5 hours.

3 Remove vegetables and chicken to large bowl using slotted spoon; keep warm. Stir water into flour in small bowl until smooth; whisk into cooking liquid. Cook, uncovered, on HIGH 10 to 15 minutes or until sauce is thickened. Serve chicken and vegetables with sauce.

Meatballs and Spaghetti Sauce

Makes 6 to 8 servings

2 pounds ground beef

1 cup plain dry bread crumbs

1 onion, chopped

2 eggs, beaten

¼ cup minced fresh Italian parsley

4 teaspoons minced garlic, divided

½ teaspoon ground mustard

½ teaspoon black pepper

4 tablespoons olive oil, divided

1 can (28 ounces) whole tomatoes

½ cup chopped fresh basil

1 teaspoon sugar

Salt and black pepper

Hot cooked spaghetti

1 Combine beef, bread crumbs, onion, eggs, parsley, 2 teaspoons garlic, ground mustard and ½ teaspoon pepper in large bowl; mix well. Form into walnut-sized balls. Heat 2 tablespoons oil in large skillet over medium heat. Add meatballs; cook 6 to 8 minutes until browned on all sides. Remove to **CROCK-POT**® slow cooker.

2 Combine tomatoes, basil, remaining 2 tablespoons oil, remaining 2 teaspoons garlic, sugar, salt and black pepper in medium bowl; stir to blend. Pour over meatballs, turn to coat. Cover; cook on LOW 3 to 5 hours or on HIGH 1½ to 2 hours. Serve over spaghetti.

 Recipe can be doubled for a 5-, 6- or 7-quart **CROCK-POT**® slow cooker.

Barbecue Turkey Legs

Makes 6 servings

Barbecue Sauce (recipe follows) | 2 teaspoons salt
6 turkey drumsticks | 2 teaspoons black pepper

1 Prepare Barbecue Sauce.

2 Season drumsticks with salt and pepper. Place in **CROCK-POT**® slow cooker. Add Barbecue Sauce; turn to coat. Cover; cook on LOW 7 to 8 hours or on HIGH 3 to 4 hours.

Barbecue Sauce

Makes about 2 cups

½ cup white vinegar | 1 tablespoon onion powder
½ cup ketchup | 1 tablespoon garlic powder
½ cup molasses | 1 teaspoon hickory liquid smoke
¼ cup Worcestershire sauce | ⅛ teaspoon chipotle chili powder

Combine vinegar, ketchup, molasses, Worcestershire sauce, onion powder, garlic powder, liquid smoke and chili powder in medium bowl; mix well.

Corned Beef and Cabbage

Makes 6 servings

2 onions, thickly sliced

1 corned beef brisket with seasoning packet (about 3 pounds)

1 package (8 to 10 ounces) baby carrots

6 medium potatoes, cut into wedges

1 cup water

3 to 5 slices bacon

1 head green cabbage, cut into wedges

1 Place onions in bottom of **CROCK-POT**® slow cooker. Add corned beef with seasoning packet, carrots and potato wedges. Pour 1 cup water over top. Cover; cook on LOW 10 hours.

2 With 30 minutes left in cooking time, heat large saucepan over medium heat. Add bacon; cook and stir until crisp. Remove to paper towel-lined plate using slotted spoon. Reserve drippings in saucepan. Crumble bacon when cool enough to handle.

3 Place cabbage in saucepan with bacon drippings; cover with water. Bring to a boil; cook 20 to 30 minutes or until cabbage is tender. Drain. Serve corned beef with vegetables; top with bacon.

Snacks and Sides

Parmesan Ranch Snack Mix

Makes about 9 ½ cups

3 cups corn or rice cereal squares

2 cups oyster crackers

1 package (5 ounces) bagel chips, broken in half

1½ cups mini pretzel twists

1 cup pistachio nuts

2 tablespoons grated Parmesan cheese

¼ cup (½ stick) butter, melted

1 package (1 ounce) dry ranch salad dressing mix

½ teaspoon garlic powder

1 Combine cereal, crackers, bagel chips, pretzels, pistachios and cheese in **CROCK-POT®** slow cooker; mix gently.

2 Combine butter, salad dressing mix and garlic powder in small bowl. Pour over cereal mixture; toss lightly to coat. Cover; cook on LOW 3 hours.

3 Stir gently. Cook, uncovered, on LOW 30 minutes.

Sauced Little Smokies

1 bottle (14 ounces) barbecue sauce

¾ cup grape jelly

½ cup packed brown sugar

½ cup ketchup

1 tablespoon prepared mustard

1 teaspoon Worcestershire sauce

3 packages (14 to 16 ounces *each*) miniature cocktail franks

Stir barbecue sauce, jelly, brown sugar, ketchup, mustard and Worcestershire sauce into **CROCK-POT**® slow cooker until combined. Add cocktail franks; stir to coat. Cover; cook on LOW 3 to 4 hours or on HIGH 1 to 2 hours.

Cheesy Polenta

Makes 6 servings

- **6 cups vegetable broth**
- **1½ cups uncooked medium-grind instant polenta**
- **½ cup grated Parmesan cheese, plus additional for serving**
- **4 tablespoons (½ stick) unsalted butter, cubed**
- **Fried sage leaves (optional)**

1 Coat inside of **CROCK-POT®** slow cooker with nonstick cooking spray. Heat broth in large saucepan over high heat. Remove to **CROCK-POT®** slow cooker; whisk in polenta.

2 Cover; cook on LOW 2 to 2½ hours or until polenta is tender and creamy. Stir in ½ cup cheese and butter. Serve with additional cheese. Garnish with sage.

Five-Ingredient Mushroom Stuffing

Makes 12 servings

6 tablespoons unsalted butter

2 medium onions, chopped

1 pound sliced white mushrooms

¼ teaspoon salt

5 cups bagged stuffing mix, any flavor

1 cup vegetable broth

Chopped fresh Italian parsley (optional)

1 Melt butter in large skillet over medium-high heat. Add onions, mushrooms and salt; cook and stir 20 minutes or until vegetables are browned and most liquid is absorbed. Remove onion mixture to **CROCK-POT®** slow cooker.

2 Stir in stuffing mix and broth. Cover; cook on LOW 3 hours. Garnish with parsley.

Macaroni and Cheese

Makes 6 to 8 servings

6 cups cooked elbow macaroni

2 tablespoons butter

6 cups (24 ounces) shredded Cheddar cheese

4 cups evaporated milk

2 teaspoons salt

½ teaspoon black pepper

Toss macaroni with butter in large bowl. Stir in cheese, evaporated milk, salt and pepper. Remove to **CROCK-POT**® slow cooker. Cover; cook on HIGH 2 to 3 hours.

 Make this mac and cheese recipe even more tasty by adding some mix-ins. Diced green or red bell pepper, peas, hot dog slices, chopped tomato, browned ground beef or chopped onion are all great options. Be creative!

BBQ Baked Beans

Makes 12 servings

3 cans (about 15 ounces *each*) white beans, drained

4 slices bacon, chopped

¾ cup prepared barbecue sauce

½ cup maple syrup

1½ teaspoons ground mustard

Coat inside of **CROCK-POT**® slow cooker with nonstick cooking spray. Add beans, bacon, barbecue sauce, maple syrup and mustard; stir to blend. Cover; cook on LOW 4 hours, stirring halfway through cooking time.

Corn on the Cob with Garlic Herb Butter

Makes 6 servings

- **6** ears of corn, husked
- **½** cup (1 stick) unsalted butter, softened
- **3** to 4 cloves garlic, minced
- **2** tablespoons finely minced fresh Italian parsley
- Salt and black pepper

1 Place each ear of corn on piece of foil. Combine butter, garlic and parsley in small bowl; spread onto corn. Season with salt and pepper; tightly seal foil.

2 Place ears in **CROCK-POT®** slow cooker, overlapping if necessary. Add enough water to come one fourth of the way up each ear. Cover; cook on LOW 4 to 5 hours or on HIGH 2 to 2½ hours.

Red Cabbage and Apples

Makes 6 servings

1 small head red cabbage, cored and thinly sliced

1 large apple, peeled and grated

¾ cup sugar

½ cup red wine vinegar

1 teaspoon ground cloves

Fresh apple slices (optional)

Combine cabbage, grated apple, sugar, vinegar and cloves in **CROCK-POT®** slow cooker; stir to blend. Cover; cook on HIGH 6 hours, stirring halfway through cooking time. Garnish with apple slices.

Honey-Glazed Carrots

Makes 6 servings

8 medium carrots (about 3 cups), cut diagonally into ⅛-inch slices

Peel and juice of 1 medium orange

2 tablespoons honey

⅛ teaspoon salt

Combine carrots, orange peel, orange juice, honey and salt in **CROCK-POT®** slow cooker; stir to blend. Cover; cook on LOW 4 hours or on HIGH 2½ hours.

Green Bean Casserole

Makes 6 servings

2 packages (10 ounces *each*) frozen green beans

1 can (10¾ ounces) condensed cream of mushroom soup, undiluted

1 tablespoon chopped fresh Italian parsley

1 tablespoon chopped roasted red peppers

1 teaspoon dried sage

½ teaspoon salt

½ teaspoon black pepper

¼ teaspoon ground nutmeg

½ cup toasted slivered almonds*

¼ teaspoon red pepper flakes (optional)

*To toast almonds, spread in single layer in small heavy skillet. Cook and stir over medium heat 1 to 2 minutes or until nuts are lightly browned.

Combine beans, soup, parsley, red peppers, sage, salt, black pepper and nutmeg in **CROCK-POT**® slow cooker; stir to blend. Cover; cook on LOW 3 to 4 hours. Sprinkle with almonds and red pepper flakes, if desired.

Channa Chat

Makes 6 to 8 servings

- 2 teaspoons canola oil
- 1 medium onion, finely chopped and divided
- 2 cloves garlic, minced
- 2 cans (about 15 ounces *each*) chickpeas, rinsed and drained
- ¼ cup vegetable broth
- 2 teaspoons tomato paste
- ¼ teaspoon ground cinnamon
- ¼ teaspoon ground cumin
- ¼ teaspoon black pepper
- 1 bay leaf

- ½ cup balsamic vinegar
- 1 tablespoon packed brown sugar
- 1 plum tomato, chopped
- ½ jalapeño pepper, seeded and minced *or* ¼ teaspoon ground red pepper (optional)*
- ½ cup crisp rice cereal
- 3 tablespoons chopped fresh cilantro (optional)

*Jalapeño peppers can sting and irritate the skin, so wear rubber gloves when handling peppers and do not touch your eyes.

1 Heat oil in small skillet over medium-high heat. Add half of onion and garlic. Reduce heat to medium; cook and stir 2 minutes or until soft. Remove to **CROCK-POT®** slow cooker. Stir in chickpeas, broth, tomato paste, cinnamon, cumin, black pepper and bay leaf. Cover; cook on LOW 6 hours or on HIGH 3 hours. Remove and discard bay leaf.

2 Remove chickpea mixture with slotted spoon to large bowl. Cool 15 minutes. Meanwhile, combine vinegar and brown sugar in small saucepan; cook and stir over medium-low heat until vinegar is reduced by half and mixture becomes syrupy.

3 Add tomato, remaining onion and jalapeño pepper, if desired, to chickpeas; toss to combine. Gently fold in cereal. Drizzle with balsamic syrup and garnish with cilantro.

Angelic Deviled Eggs

Makes 12 servings

6 eggs

¼ cup cottage cheese

3 tablespoons ranch dressing

2 teaspoons Dijon mustard

2 tablespoons minced fresh chives or dill

1 tablespoon diced well-drained pimientos or roasted red pepper

1 Place eggs in single layer in bottom of **CROCK-POT**® slow cooker; add just enough water to cover tops of eggs. Cover; cook on LOW 3½ hours. Rinse and drain eggs under cold running water; peel when cool enough to handle.

2 Cut eggs in half lengthwise. Remove yolks, reserving 3 yolk halves. Discard remaining yolks or reserve for another use. Place egg whites, cut sides up, on serving plate; cover with plastic wrap. Refrigerate while preparing filling.

3 Combine cottage cheese, dressing, mustard and reserved yolk halves in small bowl; mash with fork until well blended. Stir in chives and pimientos. Spoon cottage cheese mixture into egg whites. Cover; refrigerate at least 1 hour before serving.

Slow-Cooked Succotash

Makes 8 servings

2 teaspoons olive oil

1 cup diced onion

1 cup diced green bell pepper

1 cup diced celery

1 teaspoon paprika

1½ cups frozen corn

1½ cups frozen lima beans

1 cup canned diced tomatoes

1 tablespoon minced fresh Italian parsley

Salt and black pepper

1 Heat oil in large skillet over medium heat. Add onion, bell pepper and celery; cook and stir 5 minutes or until vegetables are crisp-tender. Stir in paprika.

2 Stir onion mixture, corn, beans, tomatoes, parsley, salt and black pepper into **CROCK-POT**® slow cooker. Cover; cook on LOW 6 to 8 hours or on HIGH 3 to 4 hours.

Buttermilk Corn Bread

Makes 1 loaf

1½ cups cornmeal

½ cup all-purpose flour

1 tablespoon sugar

2 teaspoons baking powder

½ teaspoon salt

1½ cups buttermilk

½ teaspoon baking soda

2 eggs

¼ cup (½ stick) butter, melted

¼ cup chopped seeded jalapeño peppers*

1 tablespoon finely chopped pimientos or roasted red pepper

*Jalapeño peppers can sting and irritate the skin, so wear rubber gloves when handling peppers and do not touch your eyes.

1 Coat inside of **CROCK-POT**® slow cooker with nonstick cooking spray.

2 Sift cornmeal, flour, sugar, baking powder and salt into large bowl. Whisk buttermilk into baking soda in medium bowl. Add eggs to buttermilk mixture; whisk lightly until blended. Stir in butter.

3 Stir buttermilk mixture, jalapeño peppers and pimientos into cornmeal mixture until just blended. *Do not overmix.* Pour into **CROCK-POT**® slow cooker. Cover; cook on HIGH 1½ to 2 hours.

Cereal Snack Mix

Makes 20 servings

6 tablespoons unsalted butter, melted

2 tablespoons curry powder

2 tablespoons soy sauce

1 tablespoon sugar

1 tablespoon paprika

2 teaspoons ground cumin

½ teaspoon salt

5 cups rice squares cereal

5 cups corn squares cereal

1 cup tiny pretzels

⅓ cup peanuts

1 Pour butter into **CROCK-POT®** slow cooker. Stir in curry powder, soy sauce, sugar, paprika, cumin and salt. Stir in cereal, pretzels and peanuts. Cook, uncovered, on HIGH 45 minutes, stirring often.

2 Turn **CROCK-POT®** slow cooker to LOW. Cook, uncovered, on LOW 3 to 4 hours, stirring often. Turn off heat. Let cool completely.

 Tip The Cereal Snack Mix needs to be stirred often while cooking in order to prevent it from scorching.

Everyday Desserts

Pumpkin Custard

Makes 6 servings

1 cup canned solid-pack pumpkin

½ cup packed brown sugar

2 eggs, beaten

½ teaspoon ground ginger

½ teaspoon grated lemon peel

½ teaspoon ground cinnamon, plus additional for garnish

1 can (12 ounces) evaporated milk

1 Combine pumpkin, brown sugar, eggs, ginger, lemon peel and ½ teaspoon cinnamon in large bowl. Stir in evaporated milk. Divide mixture among six (6-ounce) ramekins or custard cups. Cover each cup tightly with foil.

2 Place ramekins in **CROCK-POT**® slow cooker. Pour water into **CROCK-POT**® slow cooker to come about ½ inch from top of ramekins. Cover; cook on LOW 4 hours.

3 Use tongs or slotted spoon to remove ramekins from **CROCK-POT**® slow cooker. Sprinkle with additional ground cinnamon. Serve warm.

Rocky Road Brownie Bottoms

Makes 6 servings

½ cup packed brown sugar

½ cup water

2 tablespoons unsweetened cocoa powder

2½ cups packaged brownie mix

1 package (about 4 ounces) instant chocolate pudding mix

½ cup milk chocolate chips

2 eggs, beaten

3 tablespoons butter, melted

2 cups mini marshmallows

1 cup chopped pecans or walnuts, toasted*

½ cup chocolate syrup

*To toast pecans, spread in single layer in heavy skillet. Cook and stir over medium heat 1 to 2 minutes or until nuts are lightly browned.

1 Prepare foil handles.* Coat inside of **CROCK-POT**® slow cooker with nonstick cooking spray.

2 Combine brown sugar, water and cocoa in small saucepan over medium heat; bring to a boil over medium–high heat. Meanwhile, combine brownie mix, pudding mix, chocolate chips, eggs and butter in medium bowl; stir until well blended. Spread batter in **CROCK-POT**® slow cooker; pour boiling sugar mixture over batter.

3 Cover; cook on HIGH 1½ hours. Turn off heat. Top brownies with marshmallows, pecans and chocolate syrup. Let stand 15 minutes. Use foil handles to lift brownie to large serving platter.

*Prepare foil handles by tearing off one 18-inch long piece of foil; fold in half lengthwise. Fold in half lengthwise again to create 18X3-inch strip. Repeat 2 times. Crisscross foil strips in spoke design; place in **CROCK-POT**® slow cooker. Leave strips in during cooking so you can easily lift the cooked item out again when cooking is complete.

NOTE: Recipe can be doubled for a 5-, 6- or 7-quart **CROCK-POT**® slow cooker.

Cinnamon Roll-Topped
Mixed Berry Cobbler

Makes 8 servings

- 2 bags (12 ounces *each*) frozen mixed berries, thawed
- 1 cup sugar
- ¼ cup quick-cooking tapioca
- ¼ cup water
- 2 teaspoons vanilla
- 1 package (about 12 ounces) refrigerated cinnamon rolls with icing

1 Combine berries, sugar, tapioca, water and vanilla in **CROCK-POT®** slow cooker; top with cinnamon rolls. Cover; cook on LOW 4 to 5 hours.

2 Serve warm, drizzled with icing.

NOTE: This recipe was designed to work best in a 4-quart **CROCK-POT®** slow cooker. Double the ingredients for larger **CROCK-POT®** slow cookers, but always place cinnamon rolls on top in a single layer.

Cherry Delight

Makes 8 to 10 servings

- 1 can (21 ounces) cherry pie filling
- 1 package (about 18 ounces) yellow cake mix
- ½ cup (1 stick) butter, melted
- ⅓ cup chopped walnuts

Coat inside of **CROCK-POT®** slow cooker with nonstick cooking spray. Place pie filling in **CROCK-POT®** slow cooker. Combine cake mix and butter in medium bowl. Spread evenly over pie filling. Sprinkle with walnuts. Cover; cook on LOW 3 to 4 hours or on HIGH 1½ to 2 hours.

Cinnamon Roll-Topped
Mixed Berry Cobbler

Poached Autumn Fruits
with Vanilla-Citrus Broth

Makes 4 to 6 servings

2 Granny Smith apples, peeled, cored and halved (reserve cores)

2 Bartlett pears, peeled, cored and halved (reserve cores)

1 orange, peeled and halved

½ cup dried cranberries

⅓ cup sugar

5 tablespoons honey

1 vanilla bean, split and seeded (reserve seeds)

1 whole cinnamon stick

Vanilla ice cream (optional)

1 Place apple and pear cores in **CROCK-POT**® slow cooker. Squeeze juice from orange halves into **CROCK-POT**® slow cooker. Add orange halves, cranberries, sugar, honey, vanilla bean and seeds and cinnamon stick. Add apples and pears. Pour in enough water to cover fruit; stir gently to combine. Cover; cook on HIGH 2 hours or until fruit is tender.

2 Remove apple and pear halves; set aside. Strain cooking liquid and discard solids.

3 Dice apple and pear halves. To serve, spoon fruit with sauce into bowls. Top with vanilla ice cream, if desired.

Warm Peanut-Caramel Dip

Makes 1¾ cups

¾ cup peanut butter

1 jar (12 ounces) caramel topping

½ cup milk

Sliced apples

1 Combine peanut butter, caramel topping and milk in medium saucepan; cook over medium heat until smooth and creamy, stirring occasionally.

2 Coat inside of **CROCK-POT®** "No Dial" food warmer with nonstick cooking spray. Fill with warm dip. Serve with apples.

Spiced Vanilla Applesauce

Makes 6 cups

5 pounds (about 10 medium) sweet apples (such as Fuji or Gala), peeled and cut into 1-inch pieces

½ cup water

2 teaspoons vanilla

1 teaspoon ground cinnamon

¼ teaspoon ground nutmeg

¼ teaspoon ground cloves

1 Combine apples, water, vanilla, cinnamon, nutmeg and cloves in **CROCK-POT®** slow cooker; stir to blend. Cover; cook on HIGH 3 to 4 hours or until apples are very tender.

2 Turn off heat. Mash mixture with potato masher to smooth out any large lumps. Let cool completely before serving.

Fruit and Nut Baked Apples

Makes 4 servings

4 large baking apples, such as Rome Beauty or Jonathan

1 tablespoon lemon juice

⅓ cup chopped dried apricots

⅓ cup chopped walnuts or pecans

3 tablespoons packed brown sugar

½ teaspoon ground cinnamon

2 tablespoons unsalted butter, melted

½ cup water

Caramel topping (optional)

1 Scoop out center of each apple, leaving 1½-inch-wide cavity about ½ inch from bottom. Peel top of apple down about 1 inch. Brush peeled edges evenly with lemon juice. Combine apricots, walnuts, brown sugar and cinnamon in small bowl; stir to blend. Add butter; mix well. Spoon mixture evenly into apple cavities.

2 Pour water in bottom of **CROCK-POT®** slow cooker. Place 2 apples in bottom of **CROCK-POT®** slow cooker. Arrange remaining 2 apples above but not directly on top of bottom apples. Cover; cook on LOW 3 to 4 hours or until apples are tender. Serve warm or at room temperature with caramel topping, if desired.

 Tip Ever wonder why you need to brush lemon juice around the top of an apple? Citrus fruits, like lemons, contain an acid that keeps apples, potatoes and other white vegetables from discoloring once they are cut or peeled.

English Bread Pudding

Makes 6 to 8 servings

16 slices day-old, firm-textured white bread (1 small loaf)

1¾ cups milk

1 package (8 ounces) mixed dried fruit, cut into small pieces

1 medium apple, chopped

½ cup chopped peanuts

⅓ cup packed brown sugar

¼ cup (½ stick) butter, melted

1 egg, lightly beaten

1 teaspoon ground cinnamon

¼ teaspoon ground nutmeg

¼ teaspoon ground cloves

Apple slices (optional)

1 Tear bread, with crusts, into 1- to 2-inch pieces; place in **CROCK-POT®** slow cooker. Pour milk over bread; let soak 30 minutes. Stir in dried fruit, apple and nuts.

2 Combine brown sugar, butter, egg, cinnamon, nutmeg and cloves in small bowl; stir to blend. Pour brown sugar mixture over bread mixture; stir well to blend. Cover; cook on LOW 3½ to 4 hours or until toothpick inserted into center of pudding comes out clean. Garnish with apple slices.

NOTE: To make chopping dried fruits easier, cut fruit with kitchen scissors or a chef's knife sprayed with nonstick cooking spray to prevent sticking.

Peach Cobbler

Makes 4 to 6 servings

2 packages (16 ounces *each*) frozen peaches, thawed and drained

½ cup plus 1 tablespoon sugar, divided

2 teaspoons ground cinnamon, divided

½ teaspoon ground nutmeg

¾ cup all-purpose flour

6 tablespoons butter, cubed

1 Coat inside of **CROCK-POT®** slow cooker with nonstick cooking spray. Combine peaches, ½ cup sugar, 1½ teaspoons cinnamon and nutmeg in **CROCK-POT®** slow cooker; stir to blend.

2 Combine flour, remaining 1 tablespoon sugar and remaining ½ teaspoon cinnamon in small bowl. Cut in butter with pastry blender or two knives until mixture resembles coarse crumbs. Sprinkle over peach mixture. Cover; cook on HIGH 2 hours.

 It makes cleanup easier when cooking sticky or sugary foods when you coat the inside of the **CROCK-POT®** slow cooker with nonstick cooking spray before adding ingredients.

Pineapple Rice Pudding

Makes 8 servings

1 can (20 ounces) crushed pineapple in juice, undrained

1 can (13½ ounces) unsweetened coconut milk

1 can (12 ounces) evaporated milk

¾ cup uncooked Arborio rice

2 eggs, lightly beaten

¼ cup granulated sugar

¼ cup packed brown sugar

½ teaspoon ground cinnamon

¼ teaspoon salt

¼ teaspoon ground nutmeg

Toasted coconut (optional)*

Pineapple slices (optional)

*To toast coconut, spread in single layer in small heavy-bottomed skillet. Cook and stir over medium heat 1 to 2 minutes or until lightly browned. Remove from skillet immediately.

1 Combine crushed pineapple with juice, coconut milk, evaporated milk, rice, eggs, granulated sugar, brown sugar, cinnamon, salt and nutmeg in **CROCK-POT®** slow cooker; stir to blend. Cover; cook on HIGH 3 to 4 hours or until thickened and rice is tender.

2 Stir to blend. Serve warm or chilled. Garnish with toasted coconut and pineapple slices.

Warm Spiced Apples and Pears

Makes 6 servings

½ cup (1 stick) butter

1 vanilla bean

1 cup packed brown sugar

½ cup water

½ lemon, sliced

1 whole cinnamon stick, broken in half

½ teaspoon ground cloves

5 pears, cored and quartered

5 small Granny Smith apples, cored and quartered

1 Melt butter in medium saucepan over medium heat. Cut vanilla bean in half and scrape out seeds. Add seeds and pod, brown sugar, water, lemon slices, cinnamon stick halves and cloves to saucepan. Bring to a boil; cook 1 minute, stirring constantly. Remove from heat.

2 Combine pears, apples and butter mixture in **CROCK-POT**® slow cooker; stir to blend. Cover; cook on LOW 3½ to 4 hours or on HIGH 2 hours, stirring every 45 minutes. Remove and discard vanilla pod and cinnamon stick halves before serving.

Vanilla Sour Cream Cheesecake

Makes 6 to 8 servings

¾ cup graham cracker crumbs

¼ cup plus 3 tablespoons sugar, divided

¼ teaspoon ground nutmeg

2 tablespoons unsalted butter, melted

1 package (8 ounces) cream cheese, softened

2 eggs

¼ cup sour cream

1½ teaspoons vanilla

1½ tablespoons all-purpose flour

Fresh strawberries, sliced (optional)

Fresh mint sprigs (optional)

1 Combine graham cracker crumbs, 1 tablespoon sugar and nutmeg in medium bowl; stir to blend. Stir in butter until well blended. Press mixture into bottom and 1 inch up sides of 7-inch springform pan.

2 Beat cream cheese in large bowl with electric mixer at high speed 3 to 4 minutes or until smooth. Add remaining ¼ cup plus 2 tablespoons sugar; beat 1 to 2 minutes. Beat in eggs, sour cream and vanilla until blended. Stir in flour. Pour batter into crust.

3 Fill 6-quart **CROCK-POT**® slow cooker with ½-inch water and set small wire rack in bottom. Set cheesecake on rack. Cover top of stoneware with clean kitchen towel. Cover; cook on HIGH 2 hours.

4 Turn off heat and let stand 1 hour without opening lid. Remove lid; remove cheesecake to wire rack. Cool completely. Cover with plastic wrap; refrigerate 4 to 5 hours or until well chilled.

5 To serve, run tip of knife around edge of cheesecake and remove springform mold. Top with strawberries, if desired. Garnish with mint. Cut into wedges to serve.

Fudge and Cream Pudding Cake

Makes 8 to 10 servings

1 cup all-purpose flour

½ cup packed light brown sugar

5 tablespoons unsweetened cocoa powder, divided

2 teaspoons baking powder

½ teaspoon ground cinnamon

⅛ teaspoon salt

1 cup whipping cream

1 tablespoon vegetable oil

1 teaspoon vanilla

1½ cups hot water

½ cup packed dark brown sugar

Whipped cream (optional)

1 Prepare foil handles.* Coat inside of 5-quart **CROCK-POT**® slow cooker and foil handles with nonstick cooking spray.

2 Combine flour, light brown sugar, 3 tablespoons cocoa, baking powder, cinnamon and salt in medium bowl. Add whipping cream, oil and vanilla; stir to blend. Pour batter into **CROCK-POT**® slow cooker.

3 Combine hot water, dark brown sugar and remaining 2 tablespoons cocoa in medium bowl; stir to blend. Pour sauce over cake batter. *Do not stir.* Cover; cook on HIGH 2 hours. Turn off heat. Let stand 10 minutes.

4 Remove to large plate using foil handles. Discard foil. Cut into wedges to serve and serve with whipped cream, if desired.

*Prepare foil handles by tearing off one 18-inch long piece of foil; fold in half lengthwise. Fold in half lengthwise again to create 18X3-inch strip. Repeat 2 times. Crisscross foil strips in spoke design; place in **CROCK-POT**® slow cooker. Leave strips in during cooking so you can easily lift the cooked item out again when cooking is complete.

Coconut Rice Pudding

Makes 6 servings

2 cups water

1 cup uncooked converted long grain rice

1 tablespoon unsalted butter

Pinch salt

2¼ cups evaporated milk

1 can (14 ounces) cream of coconut

½ cup golden raisins

3 egg yolks, beaten

Grated peel of 2 limes

1 teaspoon vanilla

Shredded coconut, toasted (optional)*

*To toast coconut, spread in single layer in heavy-bottomed skillet. Cook and stir over medium heat 1 to 2 minutes. Remove from heat.

1 Place water, rice, butter and salt in medium saucepan. Bring to a boil over high heat, stirring frequently. Reduce heat to low. Cover; cook 10 to 12 minutes. Remove from heat. Let stand, covered, 5 minutes.

2 Coat inside of **CROCK-POT**® slow cooker with nonstick cooking spray. Add rice mixture, evaporated milk, cream of coconut, raisins, egg yolks, lime peel and vanilla; stir to blend.

3 Cover; cook on LOW 4 hours or on HIGH 2 hours. Stir every 30 minutes, if possible. Pudding will thicken as it cools. Garnish each serving with toasted coconut.

Hearty Vegetarian Mac and Cheese (page 82)

Index

Parmesan Ranch Snack Mix (page 133)

Metric Conversion Chart

VOLUME MEASUREMENTS (dry)

$^1/_8$ teaspoon = 0.5 mL
$^1/_4$ teaspoon = 1 mL
$^1/_2$ teaspoon = 2 mL
$^3/_4$ teaspoon = 4 mL
1 teaspoon = 5 mL
1 tablespoon = 15 mL
2 tablespoons = 30 mL
$^1/_4$ cup = 60 mL
$^1/_3$ cup = 75 mL
$^1/_2$ cup = 125 mL
$^2/_3$ cup = 150 mL
$^3/_4$ cup = 175 mL
1 cup = 250 mL
2 cups = 1 pint = 500 mL
3 cups = 750 mL
4 cups = 1 quart = 1 L

VOLUME MEASUREMENTS (fluid)

1 fluid ounce (2 tablespoons) = 30 mL
4 fluid ounces ($^1/_2$ cup) = 125 mL
8 fluid ounces (1 cup) = 250 mL
12 fluid ounces (1$^1/_2$ cups) = 375 mL
16 fluid ounces (2 cups) = 500 mL

WEIGHTS (mass)

$^1/_2$ ounce = 15 g
1 ounce = 30 g
3 ounces = 90 g
4 ounces = 120 g
8 ounces = 225 g
10 ounces = 285 g
12 ounces = 360 g
16 ounces = 1 pound = 450 g

DIMENSIONS

$^1/_{16}$ inch = 2 mm
$^1/_8$ inch = 3 mm
$^1/_4$ inch = 6 mm
$^1/_2$ inch = 1.5 cm
$^3/_4$ inch = 2 cm
1 inch = 2.5 cm

OVEN TEMPERATURES

250°F = 120°C
275°F = 140°C
300°F = 150°C
325°F = 160°C
350°F = 180°C
375°F = 190°C
400°F = 200°C
425°F = 220°C
450°F = 230°C

BAKING PAN SIZES

Utensil	Size in Inches/Quarts	Metric Volume	Size in Centimeters
Baking or Cake Pan (square or rectangular)	8×8×2	2 L	20×20×5
	9×9×2	2.5 L	23×23×5
	12×8×2	3 L	30×20×5
	13×9×2	3.5 L	33×23×5
Loaf Pan	8×4×3	1.5 L	20×10×7
	9×5×3	2 L	23×13×7
Round Layer Cake Pan	8×1½	1.2 L	20×4
	9×1½	1.5 L	23×4
Pie Plate	8×1¼	750 mL	20×3
	9×1¼	1 L	23×3
Baking Dish or Casserole	1 quart	1 L	—
	1½ quart	1.5 L	—
	2 quart	2 L	—